The Story Collector

Thirty-Three True Stories — One Ordinary Life

The Story Collector

Thirty-Three True Stories – One Ordinary Life

Bill Gurnon

Third Printing 2015

ISBN: 978-0692537831

The Story-Booker
Prior Lake, Minnesota

To order additional copies,
visit: www.gurnon.com

To Ardene

One day, the company for which I teach computer classes referred me to an elderly woman who needed some help with a writing project. Being somewhat proficient in the use of computers, I contacted this woman and arranged a meeting.

When I arrived at her home, she greeted me with boxes of memorabilia and photos from her ancestors. The volume of material was overwhelming. Her name was Ardene Neve and she said she had material enough for four books and that she needed help assembling it into book form.

After two years, Ardene had completed and printed three books before her passing in November 2014.

Ardene was a strong believer in the power of storytelling and it was her enthusiastic encouragement and endorsement that inspired me to complete the book you now hold in your hands. My heartfelt thanks go out to her.

Acknowledgements

This book would never have happened without the encouragement, enthusiasm and help of so many people - both family and friends.

First and foremost, I thank Paul Krause for inviting my wife and I to our very first, eye-opening storytelling event. I'm grateful to Don Forsberg who took on the challenge of teaching me the art of storytelling; and, to Pat Norris of Index Computers for referring me to Ardene Neve who showed me how important it is to write one's stories.

My unending gratitude goes out to Wendy Walters for her gift of time and expertise in editing this document.

Special thanks go out to Suzanne Mills-Rittmann whose peaceful cottage provided the inspiration to begin writing this book and whose encouragement kept me going.

I am awestruck by Kim Petersen's eagle eye, and grateful to her for identifying typos in the first printing of this book.

Most of all, I'm thankful for Pat's (my loving wife) continuous and enthusiastic appreciation of my storytelling (deserved or otherwise) and for her support and continuous proofing as I complete this project begun so many years ago.

Finally, none of these stories could have been told without the people who "star" in them. Their unwitting participation provided the grist for these stories, without which they would never have been created. I'm grateful for having each and every one of them in my life.

To all of you, I raise my glass and say, "Thank you!"

Bill Gurnon
November 2015

Table of Contents

Preface

I was told it would be like nothing I had ever experienced.

It all started in 1999. My wife, Pat, and I were invited to a Friday night event in Northfield, Minnesota. We were to meet in a coffee shop called Blue Monday where our friend, Paul Krause, had gathered with several people we had never met. I'm not much for talking with strangers but I trusted Paul so we went. We got coffee and sat down to a very friendly group who told us what the rules of the evening would be:

1. Everyone tells a true, personal story about a topic we all agree upon.

2. Each person is allotted 5 minutes to tell this story. A timer will be used.

3. It's expected that, as you tell your story, no one will ask questions or otherwise interrupt you. This is your time to share without competition or judgment.

We began by choosing a topic. As I recall, it was "giving." They used a timer shaped like a dairy cow to keep the time. When our 5 minutes was up, the cow timer would moo. When each of us finished our stories, the person next to us would tell their story. And so it went around the table, all of us telling a story that somehow related to "giving." After we returned home later that night, I was so energized and excited I couldn't sleep. I felt totally alive. Never before had I been allowed to tell anyone anything without being interrupted, challenged or judged. All this changed over the course of a simple 90-minute session of story sharing. Put simply, it was magical.

Since then, I've discovered, through the help of people like Paul Krause and Don Forsberg, that I have lots of stories to share. And what's more, I've learned that we all have lots of stories. The problem is we're never given a chance to share them. We live our lives, collecting stories along the way, and never, or at the most rarely, are we given the chance to pass them along.

But telling is only a fraction of the story. The major part of a story is the listening. A story isn't a story without a listener. This may seem obvious but I think it's been overlooked and underrated. Think of it this way:

A story doesn't (indeed can't) exist without a listener.

Think about your own listening habits the next time someone is sharing a story. Are you inclined to interrupt and inject your own experience? I suggest that you hold off until the person sharing with you is finished. Then, maybe they'll give you a bit more time to share your own story.

So after telling stories to friends and small audiences for more than a decade, I decided I should write some of them down. This book is a collection of those stories. They are all true. They all happened to me. I hope you enjoy them as much as I've enjoyed telling them.

I leave you with one question:

Does the person shape the story or does the story shape the person? Think about it!

Thanks for 'listening' to my stories. I hope you enjoy them.

Bill Gurnon
September 2015

Introduction

Each leaf is like a story the tree has witnessed. I see it as my calling to collect those stories.

~   ~   ~

The trees on our lot have been here a long time. I watched them grow. When we built our home on five acres of bare farmland 25+ years ago, I planted over 2000 trees there. Soon afterward, the birds and other critters moved in. We've seen foxes, coyotes, turkeys, deer (of course), possum and raccoons along with birds of all feathers including barred owls and bald eagles. The gift of trees made it all possible.

I love my trees. The only time I don't enjoy them is in the fall when I have to rake up all those dead leaves. Friends refer to our lot as Gurnon Park. Even tradesmen who come to repair a broken appliance remark how beautiful it is here. I look out over the forest we now have and watch as it changes. The trees grow and mature. Some die and stand as monuments to their gifts. Others are blown down in high winds. Still others continue to grow, providing shelter and food to all that are just passing through or to those that live here.

Owl Rest Stop

Fall brings a special beauty to the yard. Our driveway is a few hundred feet long so the walk to the mailbox takes a few minutes. The driveway is lined with maple trees and in the fall they turn spectacular shades of red and yellow.

One quiet fall day while walking down the driveway to get the mail, I heard what sounded like rain falling. I looked over at one of the maples and it was raining leaves ever so gently onto a pile already on the ground. I stood for a few minutes under that tree just listening to leaf rain. It was mesmerizing. Each leaf a story.

What joy. What peace. I took a photo and posted it on Facebook. One friend who saw it said she wanted to bring over her lawn chair and just sit under one of our trees.

I've wondered why trees are so peaceful. They live so many years and are silent witnesses to everything that happens. Despite what goes on around them, they carry on doing what they do. There's something about them that brings peace.[1]

Why do I go on about this? Because trees are witnesses to history, they make a perfect spot under which we can sit and reflect on our lives. To sit and take stock is a good thing - for us and for our family and friends. We get to know ourselves better by sharing our stories.

So bring over your lawn chair, sit under one of my trees and enjoy some of the stories I've collected.

Thanks for coming!

---

[1] I've included a poem titled "The Fall of Summer" in the Appendix of this book.

The Popsicle Thief

I grew up in a semi-rural area of Massachusetts. We had neighbors, forests, cornfields, rivers, swamps and railroad tracks. What more could a 10 year-old kid want?

One of the kids I hung around with (in those days we 'hung around,' we didn't 'hang out' or 'hang' as they do today) was Bruce. I was rather shy and rule abiding. Bruce was a bit like "let's do it first and see what happens." He was the leader; I was the follower. Bruce was like the kid named Eddie Haskell on *Leave it to Beaver*. I was the Beaver – gullible and naïve.

One summer day Bruce and I were riding our bicycles. A road maintenance crew was spraying tar on our road, and then covering it with sand. Bruce decided it would be interesting to ride onto the part of the street they'd just sprayed with wet, hot tar. I followed. Soon I realized this was not a brilliant idea and I quickly steered my bike back to dry pavement. Bruce however kept going and it wasn't long before his bike slipped on the hot, wet tar dumping him right into it. He was covered. I can't imagine what his mom said when he got home.

During that same summer, Bruce and I were out biking again. It was hot. Bruce suggested that we should ride over to the Cities Service gas station and get some refreshment. They also sold a few groceries and soda pop. I agreed this was a good idea so off we went.

When we arrived at the store we realized neither of us had any money. Bruce assured me this was not a problem. We proceeded to walk into the store and over to the freezer where they stored popsicles. Bruce

told me to pick one out. I hesitated. This is stealing! We'll
get caught. Bruce disagreed, grabbed a popsicle and
headed out the door. My eyes locked onto a root beer
popsicle (my all time favorite); my hand grabbed it and I
walked quickly, and as inconspicuously as possible out the
door behind Bruce.

Without looking back, we jumped on our bikes and sped off to a place
where we could partake of the fruits of our thievery without fear of
being caught – under the bridge, next to the river.

I ate that root beer popsicle as fast as I could and threw the stick into
the river, therefore destroying all evidence. We were never caught and,
until now, I never told anyone what I had done.

The Driving Lesson

SOME PEOPLE ARE JUST LOUD TALKERS!!! They don't mean anything by it. But they TALK LOUD. And they come across as authoritative, knowledgeable and sometimes demanding. And you know what? They can be intimidating.

Myself, I'm a quiet talker. And my wife often reminds me that I mumble. But that's the way I am. I'm just a quiet talker. Remember Leslie, the "low talker" in that *Seinfeld* episode? I'm kind of like that, but not as much.

My mom is a regular talker. She talks at a normal volume. She's neither mumbling nor talking loud. She comes across as being unassuming, thoughtful and caring. She's a regular talker.

My dad, on the other hand, he was a LOUD TALKER. And I don't know what it was about his loud talking except that he ruled our house with a firm hand. Maybe it was because he had spent time in the Navy and learned all about the chain of command and following orders. Or maybe it was just because he was a loud talker. I don't know.

I do know that when he spoke, we listened . . . and obeyed. For example, I could never stay up on Saturday nights and watch *Gunsmoke* and Matt Dillon and Doc and Chester and, of course, Miss Kitty. *Gunsmoke* was my all-time favorite TV show but I couldn't stay up and watch it except on those rare, special occasions, like the night before Easter.

My dad would say:

"Nine o'clock, Billy, time to go to bed!"

"Please, Dad, can't I watch it just this once?"

"I said, GO TO BED!"

He controlled the house and everybody in it.

I'm sure it was my dad that picked out that aluminum Christmas tree with the motorized color wheel that went wirrrh, wirrrh, wirrrh as it rotated through red, green, blue and yellow. I hated that tree. It just didn't give you that sense of warmth you get from a normal Christmas tree. You just can't get cozy with a metallic tree. But we always did what he told us to do. So every year, we put up that silver tree. Beautiful!

My sister, Carole, and
"the tree."

Yup, we always did what he told us to do:

"BILLY, CUT THE GRASS!"

"Okay."

"BILLY, SHOVEL THE DRIVEWAY!"

"Can't I wait for it to stop snowing? "

"SHOVEL THE DRIVEWAY, NOW!"

"Oh, all right."

"BILLY, CUT DOWN THE LILAC HEDGE!"

"Huh?"

Cut down the lilac hedge? I'm sure that my mom had some part in that decision. At least, I hope so. But yeah, I did have to cut down the entire, huge lilac bush. It was probably 30-40 feet long. But my dad was in charge. And my mom was just kind of in the background, you know. She must have just gone along with the flow, in her normal voice. It took weeks for me to take out that bush.

~   ~   ~

When I turned fifteen, it was time for me to get my driver's permit. And my dad, being the "best damn driver in the whole world" (according to guess who), was going to teach me how to drive. Forget about Driver's Ed. There wasn't a Driver's Ed teacher alive that could be as good as he was.

The first thing I had to learn was the "H" pattern on the gearshift for the standard transmission. All of my learning took place on **his** 1956 two-tone beige and green Plymouth Savoy that he was ever so proud of and that I had to keep clean and waxed all the time.

So we went out to the garage and he had me sit in the driver's seat while he sat in the passenger's seat. He explained the "H" pattern of the shifter and how you have to use the gas pedal in perfect synchronicity with the clutch. You push on the gas a little bit, and you let out the clutch a little bit. And you must make sure you don't let out the clutch too fast, and you don't push the gas down too much. The footwork was all very complicated. And if you get it right, the engine won't quit and the car will start moving.

Then he said, "Okay, start the engine." Now, I haven't even started the engine yet and my hands are getting all sweaty. And I'm going to have to back it out of that very narrow garage, his pride and joy that he makes me wash and wax all the time. I'm so nervous my hands are shaking.

Then he says, "Put it in reverse! Back it out." I back out the car, *very slowly* and, to my great pleasure and surprise, without any damage. Whew! He said, "Okay, that's good. Get out. We're going to go find a road where there's not much traffic."

So he drives us out to a dirt road out in the country, somewhere near Ott's Dairy Farm in North St. Paul, Minnesota, I think. I went to school with Ronnie Ott and I quietly hoped he wouldn't see me on that dirt road by his farm making a fool out of myself. My dad parked the car off to the side of the road.

He says, *"Get in the driver's seat."*

I get in the driver's seat. And I'm thinking: All right, 'H' pattern, and gas pedal, and brake pedal, and clutch.

He says, "Okay, start the engine." I start the engine.

He says, "Let's go. Put it in first." And I put it in first gear. And watching my feet very closely, I let out the clutch.

Ooooooh - we're moving! I look up. Wow! We're moving faster. I watch the front of the hood as it starts to speed past the dirt on the road. This is really cool!

He says, "Shift it into second." I look down at my feet as I let off the gas and push in the clutch when all of a sudden, around the corner comes this big truck! I think it was an oil truck and it comes right at us, like a hundred miles an hour! And it's churning up dust like crazy, and the dust is coming in the window and I'm trying not to breathe it, and Dad shouts, "LOOK OUT!" and he grabs the wheel and pulls us over to the side of the road where we stop. And he yells, "WHAT ARE YOU DOING?!? QUIT LOOKING AT YOUR FEET AND WATCH THE ROAD!!"

So ended my first lesson.

He took me on many other driving trips. One of our trips was down a four-lane road with no divider. And I'm driving in the left lane and he says, "WHY ARE YOU IN THE LEFT LANE? GET OVER IN THE RIGHT LANE. THE LEFT LANE'S FOR PASSING." Or we'd be just driving down the road and he'd say, "WATCH OUT FOR THAT KID ON THE BIKE!" Coming up to a stop sign: "MAKE A FULL STOP. ROLLING STOPS DON'T COUNT!"

My mom took me on driving trips, too. She was so different. We'd be leisurely driving along just having conversations about every day stuff like the weather or how my elderly grandmother was doing. And she'd say:

> "Now Billy, there's somebody on a bike over there, are you sure you see him?"
>
> "Yep, I'm sure, Mom. I'm fine."
>
> "Okay, that's good, Billy."

Or we'd go to the grocery store and talk about school - nothing important.

Then one day she asked me what I knew about the birds and the bees.

> She said, "Do you know how babies are made?"
>
> "Mom, I really don't want to go there!"

But she proceeded to tell me anyway. While I was driving! Groooosss and arghhhhh!!!!!!!

After several months of lessons, my dad decided I was almost ready for the driver's exam. There was just one more lesson I had to pass before going to the exam. I had to be able to make a full stop on an incline going up a hill, and then be able to start moving again. And with a standard transmission and clutch, that's a very tricky maneuver, even for an experienced driver. You have to use the brake, accelerator and clutch all at the same time and in perfect synchronization. Without a smooth transition from being stopped to moving again, you're toast – especially if someone is behind you waiting for you to get going.

So there was this place in town with a stop sign at the top of a very steep hill. The cross traffic did not stop. Boy, even with all my driving experience, I was really nervous about doing this. I tell myself over and over, watch the road. Don't look at your feet - I've learned I can't look at my feet, right?

So we get up to the stop sign, my left foot firmly planted on the clutch and my right foot solidly on the brake. I look in both directions and I freeze. I'm afraid to go. I'm afraid to go, because if I screw it up, I'll kill the engine and the car will roll backwards down the hill, crashing into that parked car back there.

"GET GOING BEFORE SOMEBODY PULLS UP BEHIND YOU!" he yells. So I pop the clutch out, the car lurches forward into the intersection but it keeps moving. The engine didn't die and we keep rolling through the intersection! Amazing! I like victories, no matter how small and insignificant.

Now that I've passed that test, it's time for my exam. We drove out to the examining station. Dad says, "Now, there's going to be a few things that you have to be sure to do in the exam." He says, "You have to make the full stops. You have to use your turn signals." And, he says with a tone of seriousness in his voice, "the examiner is going to tell you to do an emergency stop. He won't tell you ahead of time. It will not be announced. It will be a surprise. You're going to be driving along, and all of a sudden the examiner is going to say STOP!!!" Dad says, "Give it all you've got. Slam on the brakes as hard as you can, push in the clutch, and pull up the emergency brake. Do it all as fast as you can. The emergency stop, you can't screw that up."

Right. Got it.

So I get behind the wheel and the examiner slides into the front seat. He's wearing his cop-like uniform with the official "examiner" patch and a shiny badge with the seal of the State of Minnesota on it. He's not smiling - you can tell the guy's been doing this for a long time. He doesn't even look at me. I wait patiently for his instruction. He says impatiently, "Well, start the engine and let's go!" I fumble to get the keys in the ignition and start the engine. My hands are sweating and shaking, just like when I had my very first lesson. We start moving. I'm being soooo careful to make sure I make full stops at all the stop signs. I'm looking for oncoming traffic, making sure I make all the turns using the turn signal. I keep my eyes open for kids on bikes or basketballs suddenly rolling across the road. And all this time, all this time - I'm waiting for the surprise emergency stop. And it's not coming, it's just not coming. And I think it's starting to get close to the end of the test. Maybe he's not gonna do it! Could I really get through this awful test without the emergency stop? Could my dad be wrong?

And all of a sudden, he shouts, "STOP!" And just like a well oiled machine on automatic pilot . . . no wait! Just like a professional driver, I slam on the brakes, push in the clutch and pull up the emergency brake. The car stops so fast the examiner practically goes through the windshield. And the engine doesn't kill!!

Success!

The examiner turns to me and says, just like my mom in a regular voice: "You don't have to use the emergency brake."

When I told my dad what had happened, he beamed. And I have no doubt he shared what I'd done to the examiner with all his friends . . . using his LOUD TALKER voice.

Rebecca

No matter what I did, I could not get through to her. She was cold, stone-faced and indifferent. So when I look at the student roster for the adult computer class I'm scheduled to teach that day and see the name "Rebecca," my heart sinks. I want to go home and climb back into bed.

You see, I've had Rebecca in class before. She's probably in her 50s, has a round, pumpkin-like face and a sprig of pink hair sticking out from the rest of her blonde hair at the top of her head. It looks so odd I have to wonder if she knows it's there. But even more importantly, she has no facial expression whatsoever. She is stone-faced cold, like granite.

I first met her in a class I'd taught a week earlier. I had tried connecting with her (as I do with all my students), making eye contact, talking directly to her, asking her general conversational-type questions. She doesn't respond. She just stares. It was very unnerving.

During that first class, she sat next to a guy who had absolutely no experience with computers – he was a laid off truck driver. He didn't even know how to use the mouse and would move it way over into Rebecca's work area, not realizing he could simply reposition it by picking it up.

At one point during that class, I was helping the truck driver with his computer when he moved his mouse way over into Rebecca's space again accidentally bumping her workbook. She said to him in a rather harsh tone:

"Move your mouse."

He shoots back a defiant *"No."*

She repeated, more loudly now, *"Move your mouse!"*

Again he said, *"No!"*

I think to myself, things are starting to get out of control. What about the others in the class? What are they thinking?

The truck driver and Rebecca continue bickering back and forth, getting louder and louder and more impatient with each other. I thought, "I'm going to have a fight on my hands. I must _do_ something. I'm supposed to be in control here."

Finally, I said, trying to make a joke out of the whole thing, "I'm going to put someone in the time-out chair."

They stopped arguing and class resumed without further incident. Shortly afterward, we adjourned for lunch. Unfortunately, the truck driver didn't come back after lunch. Maybe he was so upset, he chose to stay away. Another satisfied customer!

Rebecca had also previously been in a different class with another instructor. After this incident, the other instructor and I were talking. She proceeded to tell me about something that happened during her class with Rebecca. As part of the lesson for this other class, students were required to set up a fictional appointment using MS Outlook, the computer calendar program. The instructor said that Rebecca had set up an appointment with "Death" in "Hell." Freaky! My skin starts to crawl. Is Rebecca a she-devil? A witch? A demon? Maybe she was just a very unhappy woman. In any case, I didn't want to find out. I hoped I'd never see her again.

But there she was, on my class roster - the class that's scheduled to start in just 15 minutes. There's no escape. I will have to face her.

So I trudge off to the classroom and begin getting the computers ready for class when in she walks. I look at her; she stares back at me. And, without thinking, I start singing:

"Good morning to you.

Good morning to you.

We're all in our places with bright smiling faces.

Good morning to you."

She just sat continuing to stare at me – never saying a word. I'm done for. And I ask myself, "What did you just do?" It's gonna be a long day.

The other students arrive and we begin our class. Later in the day, and much to my surprise, Rebecca turned to me and said, "Why do I learn more from you than from the other instructors?" I was speechless and flattered. Suddenly, her stone-faced indifference had vanished. As the class came to a close, she had become a pleasant student, one I looked forward to seeing again.

Did I finally get through to her? Maybe my silly, little song changed her.

Or maybe, just maybe, it changed me.

In College, I Learned to Play the Oven Rack

When I was in college, I learned to play the oven rack.

I was in my third year of college and needed some electives. You need a balanced program in order to earn a degree, you see. So I chose Philosophy 101. Why? I have no idea. Maybe I thought because it was a first year class it would be an easy A. Whatever the reason, there I was on the first day of class waiting for the arrival of the professor.

As he walks in and introduces himself, I notice a few things right away:

- He was tall, had short red hair, an angular jaw and spoke with a strong, German accent.
- He wore a navy blue suit with a white shirt and red tie.
- His name was Mr. Howard Smith. He was not a full professor so we didn't have to call him Dr. Smith.

And he proceeded to lay out the rules for the class. You will get an "A" in this class if you:

1. Complete the assigned reading.
2. Actively participate in class discussion.
3. Don't take notes.

Wait, what was that last one?

In fact, what he really said was:

> *"If you really want to take the best notes possible, copy the whole god-damned book!!!!"*

Now I'm no wimp when it comes to blunt language.

> But from a teacher?
>
> In the classroom?
>
> Of a state-funded university?

I wasn't at all certain I'd continue with this class.

Over the next few classes he wore the same blue suit, white shirt and red tie, and he spoke in the same harsh manner. Once, there was a guy who apparently fell asleep in class and Mr. Smith yelled out to him:

> *"Mr. Jones, get the hell out of my class."*

Do I really need to subject myself to this instructor? Surely there are other classes I could elect; other classes with less rude and intimidating instructors. I don't need this!

But here's the thing. Mr. Smith had this unusual method of teaching.

Every day he'd walk into class (always wearing the same blue suit and red tie, by the way) under the persona of the philosopher we were studying. Then we'd discuss current events with this philosopher.

One day he'd come in acting as if he were Immanuel Kant and we'd discuss racial unrest. The next day, he'd be Friedrich Nietzsche and we'd discuss student unrest.

You see, this was in the late '60s so we had plenty of stuff to talk about – civil rights, the war in Vietnam, who's the best candidate for President (Richard Nixon, Eugene McCarthy or George Wallace).

By now, it was too late to drop the class. Besides, this is starting to get interesting.

It wasn't long after I decided to stay that we had our first assignment. We had to write an analytical paper about one of the books we were reading. Now I was always a good student. After all, I was voted "most studious" in Miss Skeffington's 6th grade class.

So I worked long hours to get my first paper just right. Of course, this being a first year level class, I kind of expected I would ace this first assignment.

I turned it in, waited a few days and when I got it back Mr. Smith had scribbled comments in all the margins in bold, red ink. He wrote things like: "This is crap!" and "Rubbish." Then, at the end he wrote: "See me."

Oh great. I'm doomed. He's going to mock me and ridicule me and embarrass me just like he did that guy he threw out of class for sleeping. I'm truly screwed. At least I won't have to suffer the humiliation in front of the whole class.

So I made an appointment. And when I went to his office, he said:

> "Mr. Gurnon, the reason I berated you on your
> assignment is because you're capable of better
> thinking."

Hmmmm!!!

On my second paper, I tried even harder. Our assignment was to analyze a phrase or sentence from one of Friedrich Nietzsche's books. I chose "In music, the passions enjoy themselves." Now that I think about it, we studied a lot of German philosophers in that class. Could it be because Mr. Smith himself was German?

Anyway, when I got my second paper back, Mr. Smith had made just as many notes in the margins as on my first paper, but this time they were in blue ink. However, he still was quite blunt in his critique. He said things like: "Not well argued." and "Not well defended." and my all time favorite "Nietzsche would be embarrassed for you." Humiliation and disappointment well-up inside me. I guess I'm still not doing my best possible thinking. Then I turn to the last page.

He's written an "A." I got an "A." Can you believe it? I hardly can. Wow! Success! I met the challenge and won.

I'm starting to like this guy! I'm interested enough to take another class from him. In fact, I sign up for two more classes.

Before you know it, I decide to make Philosophy my minor (he's the only teacher in the Philosophy department).

Over the next couple of years, I take a lot of classes from him. I even seek his advice about another teacher with whom I'm having problems. He helped me apply at several graduate schools and even wrote letters of recommendation for me.

Soon, our paths begin to cross at social gatherings like Philosophy department parties and an election night get-together (the 1968 presidential election).

Then one day, Mr. Smith calls me at home!

> *"Mr. Gurnon"* (he always called me Mr. Gurnon, never Bill), *"can I come over?"*

> *"Sure!"* Why would this man I admired so much want to visit me at *MY* home?

When he arrived, he told me his teaching contract with the University had not been renewed. He would not be returning next year.

WHAT!!!!! WHY???? We can protest!!!! We'll get all your students together for a sit-in at the administration building. We can beat this! This is the '60s, after all. I'm really angry and don't want to accept this lying down.

He said, "No. That's okay. I really want to get back to Germany and my wife anyway." Then he asked me if I knew why he wore the same navy blue suit and red tie every day? He said, "It's because I try to follow their god-damned rules. But it just wasn't enough. I guess I'm too different. The administration of the University is just too conservative."

Then he said the strangest thing. "Mr. Gurnon, have you ever tried marijuana?"

> *"No."*

"Would you like to? I have some and can't take it back to Germany - they'll never let me through customs with it."

"Sure, why not?" (Remember, this was the '60s)

So he got it out and explained how to smoke it. There is a technique, you know. After about 20 minutes he asked if I felt anything yet.

I wasn't sure.

He said, "Well, there's a test you can do to find out if you're high. What you do is listen to the Beatles song "I am the Walrus." If you're stoned, you can understand the last verse. If you're not stoned, it's unintelligible."

I didn't have that record (although you can bet I went out and bought it the next day) so he said, "That's okay. There's another test. Do you have an oven rack?"

"Sure, it's in the stove" (where else would an oven rack be, right?).

"Get it," he said. What could he possibly want with an oven rack?

Then he asks, *"Do you have some shoe laces?"*

"Yes."

"Get them." And I go back to my bedroom and find a couple of old shoe laces. I don't ever throw shoe laces away unless they're broken or frayed.

"Okay."

"Now tie the shoes laces, one to each corner of the oven rack."

Got it. Done.

Finally, he says: "Grab the shoe laces with one hand and press them into your ear. Then, strum the oven rack with your other hand like you're playing the guitar. If it sounds like music, you're high."

Strum, strum, strum. "It does!!!! Like the sounds of a harp!!!"

Learning to play the oven rack wasn't the only thing I got out of college! And playing the oven rack taught me music appreciation, too.

Lost Pickles

Where the hell is that damn cat?

The cat I'm referring to started his life with us with at least a couple of strikes against him. My wife and daughter found him at a farm down the road. He was suckling on his dead mother. She had been hit by a car and was lying on the side of the road. So they asked the farmer, "What about this poor cat?" and the farmer said, "Well, he's just gonna have to look after himself." Yeah, right! My wife and daughter would have none of that. So they brought this cat home. He was in bad shape. He had parasites, he had a mouth injury of some sort, and he looked really rough. He was just a little kitten, you know, he couldn't have been more than four weeks old. And I said, "I really don't want to have another cat, I'm kinda done with animals."

"But Dad, he's hurt, we gotta take care of him."

"Okay, we'll keep him as long as we need to and get him on his feet and until he's healthy so that we can give him away to somebody."

"Okay, Dad. Thanks!"

So the next day I took him to the vet and the vet said "Well, I can give him something for the parasites, it will either kill him or cure him, we'll know by tomorrow morning." The next morning, the cat was still alive. And for that, I gotta give him some credit. Besides, he was a kitten and he was cute. He was this little blonde puff-ball sitting there with his little pointy ears and his green eyes. We named him "Pickles." And he'd do cute kitten things like sit on the kids' record player and go round and around and around, and he'd follow me outside and he'd wanna be picked up. He'd reach up putting his little paws on my leg and I'd pick him up and he'd wrap his little arms around my neck. Yeah, he was a cute little kitten. But I kept waiting for the day when I could give him away.

Well, the time got longer and longer and that day just wasn't coming. Then, one winter, one November day, kind of a cloudy and windy day, we put him outside (he always liked to go outside even when it was cold) but that night, he didn't come back. Well, I wasn't too worried about it. The next morning I went to the back door to see if he had returned, but he wasn't there. And that night, still not there. And the next morning, he *still* wasn't there. The kids are starting to get kind of worried. "Dad, where's Pickles?"

> *"Well, maybe he got lost, maybe he found another home."* (please!!!!)

> *"Well Dad, we gotta do something!"*

> *"Okay, make up a flyer that says "lost kitten" with our phone number and put it in all the neighbors' mailboxes. Maybe he'll turn up."*

But they keep nagging me about it. So finally, I said, "All right, let's go looking for him."

It's a cold, windy day and we get bundled up and we walk out into the woods calling "Pickles, Pickles." Nothing. We walk further from the house into the woods. "Pickles, Pickles." Then, I hear a very faint "Meow."

> *"Pickles?"*

> *"Meow, meow, meow."*

And we go in the direction of the meow and we find him there in a tree – maybe 20 or 30 feet off the ground, swaying in the wind with the tree.

He's way up there. "Oh, geez. You stupid cat." And the kids are telling me we must get him down or he'll die up there.

And my first reaction is, "Okay, look kids. Have you ever seen the skeleton of a cat in a tree?"

"Well no Dad, we never have."

"Well, you know why that is? Because eventually they figure out how to get down all by themselves."

"But Dad, we can't leave him up there, it's cold, it's windy, he's gonna freeze to death."

"All right."

There's only one way I'm gonna get this cat down and it's not by calling the fire department.

Tessa and Pickles

I walk back to the house and, you know, it's probably a quarter of a mile, and I get my extension ladder - my 28-foot extension ladder - and I walk back the quarter mile, carrying the extension ladder, to the cat blowing in the wind.

"Meow, meow, meow."

And I extend that ladder all the way to its maximum. And I start climbing.

"That damn cat. Why the hell does he have to be up so far?"

Now, I don't like heights. And the tree is blowing in the wind and the ladder is blowing back and forth with the cat. I really don't want to be doing this. But . . .

"Dad, you gotta rescue him, you gotta rescue Pickles."

"Meow, meow, meow."

One rung at a time, I climb the ladder while telling myself: "Don't look down!" And I get up about half way and I think, "Oh God, I'm gonna get up close to him and he's gonna get scared and he's gonna climb even higher, beyond the point where my ladder reaches."

"Don't move, you stupid cat. You just stay right there, you stupid cat."

"Meow, meow, meow."

I climb and climb. Finally, and you know the wind is blowing and somehow, I don't know how, but somehow, I get a hold of him and he puts his little arms around my neck and I start bringing him down.

"Yea, Dad. You're our hero. Yea!"

And I bring him back down to the ground and take him home.

And for the next 18 years, Pickles follows me around all over the place. When I get home from being out running errands and stuff, he'll come to the door to greet me. He'll wake me up at 4:00 in the morning just to say "meow." And he'll want company when he goes to get a drink of water. You know, he can only drink water if I cup my hand underneath the running faucet. And he'll ride on my shoulder when I walk around the backyard. He's become my best furry friend.

But as pets do, he got old and his kidneys were failing. He could barely walk, he wasn't eating at all, and he wasn't grooming himself anymore. My wife said: "He's suffering." I really wanted him to die a natural death at home but I looked up starvation on the Internet and found out that, in the final days of any living being, the body will use resources from muscle and organs to keep the brain alive. From that, I deduce that he's fully aware of his discomfort and pain. And, as my wife said, he was suffering.

So I made the extremely difficult decision to put him down.

The vet was great about it. They gave us as long as we needed to say goodbye. And we were in a dimly lit, quiet and private room. It couldn't have been more peaceful. When I was ready to let go, the vet came in to get him. Pickles gave one last hiss at the vet and that was the last I saw of him. We went out to the car to wait and when they brought him out, his body was in a small, shoe-like box. We drove home in silence.

It was winter at the time and the ground was frozen so I couldn't bury him right away. I decided I would store his remains in the freezer until he could be buried in the yard. When I took the box out of the car and walked toward the house, I noticed it was still warm from what remained of his body heat. So sad . . .

~   ~   ~

That spring, I pulled him out of his temporary resting place in the freezer. And I dug a hole in the front yard. And I put him in there, covered him up and said my goodbyes.

I'm finally rid of that damn cat (said while secretly sobbing).

No More Plumbing!

My wife, Pat, said to me: "Bill, I don't want you to do any more plumbing around this house." This wasn't necessarily bad news.

~   ~   ~

I had decided to undertake a massive project, massive to my mind, anyway. I was going to put a shut-off valve on every single sink and every single toilet in our house. This seemed to me a good thing to do, 'cause you know, if a toilet breaks, and you don't have a shut-off valve on it, you have to turn off the water to the entire house. So every toilet and every sink needs a shut-off valve, right? I knew you'd agree.

So, I'm well into this project. It's coming along quite nicely, thank you very much. And on the last day, a Sunday afternoon, I'm working on the final toilet. And I'm working at getting the pipe off, and it's a little bit stuck, a little bit harder than some of the others. And I lean into it a little bit, and it ain't moving. So I give it everything I've got. And all of a sudden, BAM! Shwwwwsssssh! I'm not seeing water, but I can hear it. The pipe has broken - *INSIDE* the wall.

Uh oh.

I run downstairs as fast as I can, look for the water main and shut off the water to the entire house. Then I go look underneath the wall where the toilet is located - it's like rain coming down in there. This is not good. To fix this, I would to have to put a hole in the wall this big. It ain't gonna happen.

So I go upstairs and tell Pat, "I had a small problem, I had to turn off the water to the house, I broke a pipe in the wall. It's Sunday afternoon, I know, but I'll call a plumber tomorrow and we'll get it all taken care of."

Needless to say, she's not happy and she objects:

> "Tomorrow? No way! We can't wait till tomorrow. I've got kids in diapers! I've got to take care of this tonight."
>
> I say, "We can't get a plumber - even if we can get a plumber on Sunday afternoon, it's going to cost a small fortune."
>
> She says, "Don't worry about it, I'll get a plumber. I'll take care of it. But you know," she says, "I don't want you to do any more plumbing."

~   ~   ~

A few years after that, we built a new house. I didn't care about anything else in this new house, except I wanted every sink and every toilet to have its own shut-off valve. So I told the builder, I said, "Here's my only requirement . . ." And he remembered.

And after the house was built and we were moved in, every once in a while I'd do my little tour of toilets. Look at that shut-off valve. Nice, huh? It felt so good to have shut-offs on all of those toilets.

One day I went downstairs and was looking behind a toilet and there's a little drip coming off of that valve. Remembering what Pat said: "You'll do no more plumbing around this house," I go up to the kitchen, and I find the plumber's friend: a small, plastic Tupperware bowl. And I go back downstairs and I very professionally put it right underneath the leak. And it drips into the bowl very nicely. And I check it from time to time, and I empty it when I need to. Hey - this 'no more plumbing' thing is working pretty well.

~   ~   ~

One afternoon, some time later, I looked out into the backyard. We have an above-ground swimming pool, it's about four feet high. I take pride in this pool. I work hard at getting the water clean and ready for swimming, or for just looking at - you know, it sparkles in the sun. And I'm looking out at the pool, and the water level is about eight inches too low - oh my gosh! I run outside, there's water pouring out all over the place. What's going on?

My beautiful pool! My beautiful, clean water is draining out into the backyard!

I quickly figure it out and I know what I need to do, at least temporarily. I reposition a filtration hose to stop the water from draining into the backyard. So I got that taken care of. I surveyed the damage and figured out in short order that what had happened was that part of the filtration system had broken. The cover on the strainer had broken off. Fixing this is not something I wanted to do this weekend, but I've got to take care of it quickly. You see, if you don't circulate pool water, it turns into a swamp and the ducks move in.

So I call Pat, who was at work. I say, "Can you go over to the pool store on the way home from work, and just pick up a new strainer? Ours broke, we lost eight inches of water . . ."

She says, "Oh sure, I'll be happy to." So she brought it home, and she says, "How are you going to put that on?"

I said, "I don't know. I'll worry about that tomorrow."

So Saturday morning comes along, a beautiful sunshiny day. I wake up and have my cup of coffee. I decide I'm going to put myself in the right frame of mind to do this project. I'm going to take a walk around Cleary Lake. So I go out, walk around the lake. People are happy, they're saying "hello" to me, and I'm saying "hi" back. I'm thinking, this is a good sign. I know this is a plumbing project, but it's going to go okay. I think it's going to work out.

I get back home and proceed to take the old, broken strainer off, and I put the new one on. And you know, strainers have a top and a bottom.

I put the new one on, and strangely, the top was on the bottom. And I'm not real smart, but I thought, this isn't right. So I figured I must have done something wrong. It must be my fault. It couldn't be the pool manufacturer's fault. This is a beautiful pool. It's a Hayward pool. When we bought it, the guy told us it was the "top of the line."

So this must be my problem, I must have put it on upside-down. So I took it off, and I tried to get it so that it would be right side up. It wasn't going to go. It was upside down, every single time. So I thought, "Let me just take this apart a little bit further." And I took off a few more screws. And oops, what's that? Something fell out: another broken part. Good grief!

Just then, Pat opens the patio door. She says, "Hi Billy! How's it going?" I go up to the house, and I explain my woes. And she says, "That's okay. We'll just go to the pool store this afternoon, we'll get the part, we'll get it taken care of." She's so optimistic about this.

Well, okay. So we go to the pool store that afternoon. And I buy the new part - the one that fell off onto the ground. I say, "You know, by the way, that strainer that we bought, I can't get it on so that the top is on the top. The top is always on the bottom."

The pool guy says, "Oh, just take some Teflon tape and wrap it around there." He says, "Put a big wad of Teflon tape on that thing, and that'll hold it."

I said, "Now wait a minute. This is a Hayward pool. It's supposed to be top of the line." This just seemed like a rinky-dink solution for something that's "top of the line."

The pool guy says: "Hayward, huh. Well, that's a piece of junk."

~   ~   ~

When my wife speaks, I listen. I only wish she had told me not to do outside plumbing either.

At least the ducks still appreciate the "piece of junk."

KDWB, Trick or Treat!

Did you ever do anything stupid when you were a teenager?

I was a fairly normal 15 year-old. I got good grades in school, obeyed my parents and had friends who didn't do stupid things. I was normal. Well, mostly normal anyway.

You see, I really enjoyed listening to my favorite radio station, KDWB. I'd listen from the time I got home from school until the time I went to bed. I was almost more interested in radio than I was in girls - almost. I'd even make my own tape recordings pretending that I was the radio announcer. I idolized those guys. But it wasn't just radio in general. It was KDWB! They were the best. You may remember it: "KDWB, Channel 63. That's Easy to Remember."

They played all my favorite rock 'n' roll songs. And the DJs seemed to talk directly to me, like I was the only one listening.

That Halloween, KDWB was having a contest and the winner would receive a free radio! And, while it would have been really cool to win a new radio, participating in this contest would have been another way in which I could be connected, even become a part of, KDWB. So, I decided to play the game and try winning that radio. The only catch was you had to go knocking on doors of houses only within the city limits of St. Paul and I lived in Maplewood and was too young to drive. The contest required that you knock on the door, say "**KDWB, trick or treat**" and, if you knocked on the door of the winning house, you'd win the radio. Sounds easy! I started making my plans.

First of all, I wasn't going to tell anyone about it. How embarrassing it would be telling my mom that I was going trick or treating - at age 15! And, my friends would think I'm stupid believing that I could actually win a radio by knocking on a door. St. Paul does have a lot of houses! So I didn't tell anyone what I was going to do. I would only tell them if I won.

The evening of Halloween arrives and I tell my mom I'm going out. Since I'm too young to drive, I have to walk to the city limits of St. Paul - about two miles away (not a big deal to a 15 year-old). It's Halloween. It's dark. It's end-of-October cold, and it's starting to drizzle. And two miles becomes a long way to walk in the drizzly dark, on Halloween.

So I start out and the first couple of blocks are easy - street lights and familiar houses. Kids are out trick or treating. I'm in safe territory. But then I cross the road. There's a big, dark, empty golf course on one side of the road, and only a few houses on the other. Then, just a swamp and a forest. It's dark. Really dark. I'm listening to the sound of drizzle and wind and silence in the woods. I think I hear something. I look around for suspicious activity. Is there someone behind that storage shed? What was that over there? I'm kind of scared. Someone could be lurking in the darkness. A vicious and cruel evil-doer waiting for me to pass by. Waiting to jump out at me and beat me up or kidnap me. I walk faster, looking down. Maybe if I don't look, the evil-doer won't come after me.

Finally, I cross the railroad tracks and into a neighborhood. Once again, the kids are out trick or treating. I'm back in civilization. Whew. I've arrived in St. Paul. I'm safe.

Now my work begins. Now I start knocking on doors.

"KDWB Trick or Treat!"

"What?"

"KDWB Trick or Treat!"

"Huh?"

"Oh, it's a contest," I explain. "I'm going around St. Paul knocking on doors and saying: "KDWB Trick or Treat!" in hopes of winning a radio."

"Oh. Well, we don't have a radio but would you like some candy?"

"Sure!"

On to the next house.

"KDWB Trick or Treat!"

"What?"

I explain again, feeling a little embarrassed.

"Oh. We don't know anything about it. Would you like some candy?"

"Sure."

Next house, same routine. My pockets are filling up with candy and it's becoming more and more embarrassing with each house.

Finally, after only five houses (out of how many in St. Paul?), and total embarrassment, I give up and head home.

Once again, walking as quickly as I could, past the very dark swamp and woods where the scary evil-doer lurked. But now I'm feeling more stupid than scared compared to my earlier trip past this place.

It's been drizzling this whole time and so by the time I get home, I'm soaked. My mom doesn't say anything, thank goodness. I go upstairs to my bedroom and don't tell anyone about it.

Did you ever do anything stupid when you were a teenager? I sure did!

Two Young Boys and One Grumpy Old Man

I ask myself: "Am I a grumpy old man?"

When my wife and I bought five acres of farmland about 25 years ago, I immediately began to fill it with trees - over 2000 of them, all seedlings. Just babies, really, planted all over the 5 acres in hopes of becoming a grown-up forest someday. I even made a walking trail through the trees so that anyone could stroll past them and enjoy the space they were creating.

Over the first few years, my babies continued to thrive and grow. And I would take my semi-annual walk around the trail encouraging each little tree as it grew taller and wider. It didn't take too long before they were nearly as tall as me.

Then we got new neighbors - with two young boys. Two young boys who had go-carts. And what seemed to me to be too-little adult supervision. One time I caught one of the boys racing his go-cart around the trail I'd made through my pre-mature forest. Not only was this kid trespassing on my private property, he could have easily run over and killed one or more of my trees. I quickly ran outside and told him to stop. Then, I called his dad and he assured me the boy would never do that again. I was pleased with the father's response but apprehensive about the future. So I kept a close eye on these kids. I would never let anything like this happen again, not on my watch!

Well, my keen observation (or was it spying?) paid off.

It was a cool and windy fall day. You know the kind - after everything has turned brown but before the snow falls. It was cloudy, too. And I was hoping for rain since we hadn't had any for a while and my trees were thirsty. That's when I saw them - the two young boys were heading into their backyard very close to the property line – my property line. What were they up to now? I kept an eye on them. Suddenly, I saw smoke. Holy crap. They've started a fire! How could they be so stupid as to start a fire on this windy day when the brush and everything is so dry? They could start my entire yard on fire! Those idiots.

I ran as fast as I could out the door and down my trail. I ran over to them as they sat around the fire and yelled, "What are you trying to do?" They sheepishly replied, "We're just having a little camp fire." Their faces were full of innocence – like little kids. "You can't have a fire on a day like today. Are you crazy?" And I stomped the fire out with my foot. I guess I showed them.

I walked slowly back to the house casually looking at my shoe to see if it was burned. I wasn't in the house more than 2 minutes when the phone rang. It was the boys' father. In the fraction of a second it took before he could put me in my place, I realized what I had done. I apologized and I told him it was wrong of me to yell at his boys and put out their fire.

I can still see their innocent faces. I really don't want to be a grumpy old man. Do you think I am?

The backyard saved from the ravages of fire.

The Deer

Life can get a little same-y sometimes. Know what I mean?

I was on my usual same walk around the same lake passing the same people looking at the same squished worms on the same paved trail. I could probably do that walk with my eyes closed. Sometimes I wish I could walk with my eyes closed so I could think about stuff or even meditate. The danger to that would be that I wouldn't be able to see the inevitable pile of doggie doo and would step right into it. So I keep my eyes open.

I recently saw a woman walking the same trail backwards! I was very impressed.

Walking is a creative activity for me. I have some of my best ideas while walking. Like the time I had the idea for a new website, one that I was sure would rival YouTube in popularity. So far, Google has not come forward with an offer to purchase my website, however. That's okay. I can wait. The longer they wait, the higher the price.

But on this particular walk, I wasn't thinking about anything in particular, I was just trying to avoid all the worms that had come out after a recent rain. It was a weekday so there weren't even any of the same people I normally see. I was pretty much all by myself. Or, so I thought.

As I rounded a curve in the trail, I noticed a deer up ahead. This is not unusual for the park. Deer abound here, so much so that every fall, the park holds a bow and arrow deer hunt. Usually when I see deer, they just turn and run away with their white tails pointing straight upward. Not this time. This deer stood her ground. I continued to approach her but now was walking as slowly and quietly as I could. Since she was just staring at me, I wanted to see how close I could get before spooking her. She was standing only about 12 or 15 feet from the trail (about 50 feet from me) as I approached.

I crouched down and continued to move in squatting position towards her. She just stared; not moving except for an occasional stomping of her front hoof.

Finally, when I was only about 20 feet from her, I said "Hi. Don't be afraid. I won't hurt you." That was all it took. She turned and moved away but still stayed relatively close. I couldn't crouch any longer and I needed to get back to my office so I stood up and began walking again. As I passed her, I turned around to say goodbye and that's when I saw them. On the opposite side of the trail were two fawns, young enough to still have speckled coats. I had gotten between them and their mom.

And, here I thought it was _me_ she was interested in.

Step, Step, Step

It was a dark and stormy night. Really!

When I was about eight years old my family lived in Massachusetts. We had a small house in a rural neighborhood and my brother and I shared an upstairs bedroom. The bedroom was at the end of one large, open space on the second floor. I know you've seen the style - a window on each end. Our bedroom was on the far end opposite the stairs. There was a chimney on one wall of our bedroom and a window on the other. In the photo, the bedroom was on the right side of the house next to the chimney.

It had been raining when we went to bed but I went to sleep right away. The sound of a steady rain is so relaxing, isn't it?

Sometime in the middle of the night I woke to a noise. It sounded like someone was walking up the stairs; step, step, step. Who could it be?

It was pitch dark; I couldn't see anything. But there's that sound again. Step, step, step. Could it be one of my parents?

Step, step, step. Why would they be coming up the stairs at this hour?

Step, step, step. Or could it be a stranger? Could someone be in our house? Could it be some evil person - a robber maybe?

My brother was still asleep. I resented him for it.

Step, step, step.

By now, I was freaking out. I was certain it was a robber come to take who knows what valuable items from my room. There was, after all, my piggy bank with at least $2.47 inside. Or maybe, just maybe, he was there to kill me.

Step, step, step.

I tried to shout out for my mom but the words just wouldn't come. It was like I had no breath to shout with. But I kept trying. Finally, I was able to get out a long and loud MOOOOOOOOOOOOM! And again, MOOOOOOOOOM!

Both my parents came running.

> *"Billy, what's the matter?"*

> *"There's a robber coming up the stairs."*

> *"We didn't see anybody."*

> *"I can hear him walking. Can't you hear it? I can still hear him."*

Step, step, step.

That's when my dad looked down at the base of the chimney at the end of our bedroom. Coming out of the chimney base was a small pipe and positioned under the pipe was an empty coffee can. It was there to catch the drips of rain coming down the chimney.

My dad looked at me and pointed at the pipe. I looked at the drops of rain falling into the coffee can. Drip, drip, drip.

"Oh. Never mind."

Trapped

It was grand.

My wife and I had just moved into this huge, gorgeous house. Our friends were totally impressed. It had over 3200 square feet with five bedrooms, three bathrooms, two living rooms and 20 x 25 foot master bedroom with huge windows and a multi-level

deck. It was surrounded by so many trees you could sunbathe in the nude and not be seen by anyone. You can see the large bedroom windows to the left above the garage in the photo.

It was grand. Clearly, we had made it to the big time. We were successful and now our house proved it.

We had moved into this palace in October, just before winter. And, it was shortly afterward that someone else did, too. Every night, you could hear them scratching in the walls. Mice!

Mice! Scratching away, probably eating electrical wires or something. Keeping us awake what seemed like all night long. I will fix this problem. I've dealt with mice before. I'm experienced. All I need are the right tools. With the right tools, you can fix anything.

So, the next day, I go to the hardware store to pick up some mousetraps. To my surprise, someone has invented a better one – one that has a trigger mechanism in the shape of cheese! And the package says "no bait needed" so I guess it smells like cheese, too. I buy a package of these marvelous new devices and head home with high hopes of conquering this problem in very short order, now that I have the right tools.

As I mentioned, our bedroom was over the garage so it will be relatively easy to set traps inside the garage and near the walls where we've been hearing the midnight scratching. I prepare all four traps but I'm not taking any chances. I add my own secret bait to the fake cheese. If you promise not to tell anyone, I'll share it with you. Promise? Okay, it's peanut butter. Mice love it, especially the creamy, smooth type. They're not so keen on the crunchy style. I guess it's too hard to chew or something. And it has to be the Jif brand. Skippy just won't do. Then we wait until dark; our heads hit the pillows; and we listen; and we wait. We wait for the scratching.

But it never comes. We sleep uninterrupted all night. Nice!

Eager to see what I've caught overnight, I get dressed first thing in the morning and check the garage for bounty. Sure enough, one of the traps has captured a night marauder and is lying on the garage floor. I pick up the trap and dump the dead mouse unceremoniously into the garbage can; dirty little bugger. I reset the trap and put it back in place.

After another peaceful night, I check the traps again. Again, I am successful. Another one has bit the . . . fake cheese. I'm feeling pretty good about all this. This must be how successful hunters feel after a kill. I can now relate.

This continues for some weeks. I'm beginning to wonder where all these mice are coming from. When will it end? The garbage man must be wondering why the can is always filled with dead mice.

Then, one weekend day, I perform the routine, again. And as always, when I get to the garage, there's a trap on the floor with a mouse attached. I reach down to pick it up . . . and the mouse looks back at me. He's still alive!

This changes everything. What am I going to do now? I can't just throw him into the garbage. I'm going to have to put him out of his suffering. I'm going to have to kill him myself, directly. Person to mouse, I'm going to have to put an end to his life. The trap didn't do its job completely so now I have to finish it. And, I'm no good at this. I don't want to be good at this. I know it from when I was a teenager and had to end the life of a bird that had been hit by a car. I hated doing it. Only thing I could do was to drive my car over it. At least that way I didn't have to look at it.

But now I will have to look. How am I going to do this so it's painless for both of us? I could hit him with a hammer. No, that's too up close. I need to be farther away. Besides, what if I missed?

I could drop him into a bucket of water and let him drown. Nope. Drowning would cause more suffering.

I've got it.

I grab the trap with the mouse hanging from it and a shovel from the garage. We walk to the backyard where there are some large rocks. I place the trap/mouse on one of the rocks. He looks at me again. I tell him I'm sorry, close my eyes, raise the shovel and strike at the mouse as hard as I can. I open my eyes to see if my shovel was on target. It was. The mouse has died. I've performed my duty.

I turn and look up at our house. It doesn't seem quite so grand anymore.

Where is Mom?

My sister laughed when we gave my mom her Christmas gift.

When my mom was in her 80s, she lived in a mother-in-law apartment in my sister's house. She didn't get out much and spent every day watching old movies on television. So I thought it would be a good idea to get her a small, uncomplicated DVD player. I made sure it would be low-tech and easy to use, sort of  like some microwave models that still have turn dials. I understand how difficult it can be for older folks to grasp technology. After all, how many of us know what every button on that remote does anyway, right? I sure don't.

~ ~ ~

Flash back to when I was a kid. My mom and dad would often argue. I never knew what the arguments were about - I would always just go to my room and close the door. I do know that my mom would always stand up for what she believed in. Always. Nobody could bully her, that's for sure, not even my loud, brash father.

I remember one specific occasion when the argument was so heated that my mom walked out the door, hopped into the car and drove away. I was quick to follow on my bike. Thankfully, she was driving slowly, probably because she was crying so much. As I rode my bike beside the car, I pleaded with her through the open window not to go. I begged her to stay. Finally, she stopped the car and agreed to come back home. They divorced soon afterward. My mom knew how to stand up for her rights.

~　　　~　　　~

But now it's years later at Christmas time and we're all gathered around my mom's living room opening gifts. Remember the perfect gift I bought her – the low-tech DVD player? I was very pleased with myself for being so thoughtful. But when mom opened my special gift, my sister (along with her husband), laughed and made fun of it. They said there was no way mom would be able to use it. I strongly disagreed and vigorously defended my choice. At least mom should try it out for a while to see if she liked it. Give it a chance!

During this entire discussion, mom didn't say anything. She didn't stand up for herself at all. What ever happened to that woman who stood up to her unpleasant husband? She just quietly sat there as they made fun of my gift. I couldn't believe it.

She never used the DVD player. In fact, she didn't even want to try it out. She thanked me and gave it back.

Mom, where did you go?

This photo of a magazine cover shows me (at four months old) and Mom as we board a train going from Minnesota to California.

And That's the Way it Was . . .

Uh, oh.

East Bridgewater, Massachusetts 1957. I'm in Miss Sawyer's 5th grade class and it's movie time. I always loved movies in school. Movie time meant that, when the lights went out, you could do stuff and not get caught. I never actually did any stuff to get caught with, but it was fun thinking that I could. There was a feeling of freedom when those lights went out. And for a pre-adolescent in the 5th grade, that was big.

And so it was when it came time for us to watch an episode of Walter Cronkite's *You Are There*. Walter would tell us about a day in history, describing it (with the aid of performers acting out the scenes) in such great detail that you'd feel like you really were there. We all had to gather in the assembly room – a large, open space with dark shades drawn and rows of wooden chairs, all with wooden seats and wooden slats on the back. I sat towards the back of the room, like always. You have more freedom to do stuff in the dark when you sit in back.

So the lights go out and the movie starts and Walter starts talking about that day in history when the Declaration of Independence was signed. And I sit back in my wooden chair to get comfortable and promptly slide my elbow through the wooden slats on the back. I try to pull it out and it won't budge. Uh, oh. That's weird. It slipped in so easily. Maybe if I just twist it a bit. Nope. It's stuck. Oh, great. Now what?

So here I am, stuck to the back of my chair trying to watch my second favorite person on TV, Walter Cronkite (the Lone Ranger was my first favorite). Walter's going on about the people at the signing of the Declaration of Independence. And I really do want to watch. But I'm kind of too busy twisting and pulling my arm trying to extricate my elbow from the back of my chair. No matter how hard I pull and no matter which direction I pull in, it won't budge. And this is only a half-hour movie. I don't have a lot of time. I start getting all sweaty and nervous.

Then it occurs to me. What if I'm caught? What if the lights come on and all the kids stand up and I don't 'cause I'm stuck in the stupid chair? What if Miss Sawyer, my favorite teacher (and first crush of my entire life), sees me? I loved Miss Sawyer. I can't be seen like this, looking like an idiot who got his elbow stuck in his stupid chair. I'm such a dope!

And, what if the lights come on and I'm still stuck and they have to call the janitor to get me out; or worse yet, even the fire department? I can see it all now. All the kids are standing around laughing at me while the fire fighters, decked out in full fire-fighting gear, come running into the room pulling loaded fire hoses behind them ready to combat the worst eventuality. And then there's Miss Sawyer, standing on the sidelines just watching, an expression of huge disappointment on her face. And if that's not enough, when my dad finds out he is gonna be sooooo mad. He'll kill me, for sure.

I twist and pull some more. Um, um, um! It's really starting to hurt a lot. Still nothing. Walter is starting to wrap it up. He's telling us that the document has been signed and everyone is congratulating each other. Pull and twist, twist and pull. Um, um, um! Ouch, ouch, ouch! I'm gonna get out of this no matter what I break in the process. Walter says, "And that's the way it was . . ." and with every ounce of strength I have left, I grit my teeth and give one final yank and POW! My elbow comes free just as the lights come on.

Nobody ever knew what happened, least of all Miss Sawyer. Somehow, movies have never been quite the same.

Author's Note: This story was broadcast on Minnesota Public Radio as part of its first Story Slam in July 2007. The topic was "Escape." You can listen to it here:

http://gurnon.com/Samples.html

Beartooth Pass

Moms can be very helpful even when you want them to be. You heard me. My mom was helpful. In fact, I *asked* for her help.

It was June and my friend Pat and I were planning a road trip in my

1975 VW Beetle from Minneapolis to Seattle. And this was in the BC era – Before Computers. Knowing that my mom was a member of the AAA auto club (known as "triple A"), I asked her if she would request a "trip-tic." Now for those of you

The road to Beartooth Pass

who are younger than 40, a trip-tic is triple A's map service which provides a complete map of whatever driving trip you're planning. And the trip-tic from Minneapolis to Seattle was several pages long each with a map showing the purple-highlighted route they recommended. They even provided points of interest along the way. And it was one these particular points of interest (Beartooth Pass in Montana) which intrigued me. It was described as spectacular, "a must see." CBS's Charles Kuralt described it as "the most beautiful drive in America." And this destination was along our way to Seattle. We had to see it!

But alas, our trip going west was marred by an overcast sky and rainy weather. It was so gray and gloomy that when we arrived at the point in the road where we'd have to exit to get to Beartooth Pass, we decided to postpone and hope for better weather on the return trip.

However, as bad luck would have it, weather on the return trip was no better. We reasoned that we might never get by this way again so we decided to take the exit and see what we could see despite the rain.

We filled up the tank with gas and headed for the mountain. The highway took us into Yellowstone Park but we didn't see anything noteworthy there. And it was raining so we didn't feel like stopping.

As we began heading ever so gradually up the mountain, we passed an open gate with a large sign reading:

"SNOW CHAINS REQUIRED BEYOND THIS POINT"

But since it was the 12th of June, we knew it didn't apply to us although I did wonder why they wouldn't take the sign down over the summer months.

We continued our leisurely drive. Our destination was Red Lodge, Montana. It was early Sunday evening and after driving all day, we were eager to get to our motel. The light rain continued. It was so dark and gloomy, I never even thought to stop and take a photo of this spectacular countryside.

Then, I thought I noticed a tiny speck on the windshield. Then another. But just as quickly as they hit, they were gone. Hm. Pat didn't say anything so apparently either I was just seeing things or she didn't see it. There were only two of them – specks that is. Tiny ones. Could they be bugs? I don't think so. They disappeared too quickly. Could they be . . . ?

We continued slowly up the mountain, turning left around the hairpin turns you picture as one drives up the side of a mountain. Again, I see some specks of something on the windshield; a few more of them now. And they disappear just as quickly. But more appear just as quickly as the others disappear. I don't want to think what I'm thinking. It is June after all. Could this be sn . . . ? No. Don't say it. I can't say it or even think it. If I were to think it or say it, it might come true. I put my best effort into ignoring the tiny specks of mysterious material. And I can ignore stuff pretty well when I put my mind to it.

All of a sudden, Pat says "Is that snow?" NO, DON'T SAY IT OUT LOUD! Oh man, now she's jinxed it. So, at first I try faking it like I don't know what she's talking about.

"What? Snow? Are you crazy? It's June!"

But then I look around outside the car and I see them; flakes of wintery white stuff floating in the rain. There's not a lot of it but it's undeniable. There's snow in the air. Oh well. How bad could it be? Just keep driving and everything will be fine.

I steer into another hairpin turn and suddenly we're surrounded by snow, not just in the air but also on the road - several inches of it! Oh shit! I look down at the gas gauge thinking we should turn back. The tank is less than half full and there hasn't been a gas station since the one we filled up at when we pulled off the freeway to come here.

Now it's important that you understand what a 1975 VW Beetle (the car we're traveling in) is like. First off, mine is blue, the color of cold. It sits close to the ground. I've gotten stuck trying to drive over just a few inches of snow back home in Minnesota. And it has no heat to speak of. In fact, the only heat you get is when the car is moving. When it's not moving, you get diddly-squat.

We turn another hairpin curve and now we're in a full blizzard with at least 8 inches of snow on the road. Thank God for the Winnebago just ahead of us. Without those tire tracks in the snow, we'd be stranded for sure. I resolve to keep my foot on the accelerator, no matter what. Stopping now would be a life and death mistake. We keep moving forward. There's nothing to see but snow - with mountainside to the left of us and sheer nothingness to the right (they don't even put guardrails on the nothingness side). We must be near the summit although we can't see anything. I keep my eyes focused forward, my foot on the gas. I was convinced that to be stranded without food or heat on the top of this mountain on a Sunday evening in June would be fatal. They'd send a helicopter looking for survivors and find exactly none.

Pat is starting to get really tense and she's asking me all kinds of stupid questions like:

"What are we going to do?"

"How will we get down?"

I don't answer. When I'm stressed, I stop talking. I'm totally focused on keeping a forward motion.

We turn into another hairpin curve and, miraculously, the snow abates. Now it's a mix of snow and rain. Another turn and now it's just rain again. I breathe a silent sigh of relief (can't let Pat know how frightened I was).

We continue down the mountain and reach Red Lodge well after dark. We see a gas station right next to our motel. I'll fill up there in the morning. At the motel, Pat says, "Should we call the highway patrol? What if someone gets stranded up there?" I agree this is a good idea. I place the call and tell the dispatcher about the blizzard and the impossible road conditions. He just laughs and says, "Oh, that road's closed."

So much for "the most beautiful drive in America."

Women, Ey!

Okay guys, let's admit it. Women have a lot of influence on us.

Listen. We're all friends here, right? Can I be honest with you? I gotta get this off my chest.

~   ~   ~

I blame my wife, Pat, for everything. In fact, I blame women in general.

First, there's Linda . . .

It all started back in 1993. I got an invitation in the mail from a woman I had long forgotten about – Linda Bowers (now Linda Bowers-Smith). My high school choir director (Carl Lipke) was retiring and she was getting some alumni together to sing at his final school concert. I ignored the letter. Then, she called me. I told her I wasn't interested, but she talked me into it saying that Warren Tracy, Jon Juehrs and Dick Ferrazzo - all my old high school friends would be there. So I went.

The first rehearsal was in the same room in which we had rehearsed in high school. The walls were the same off-yellow color, the chairs were lined up in the same way and it still smelled of the boys locker room down the hall. And Mr. Lipke, the choir director, looked the same, too! He hadn't aged. I loved it. All my memories of singing in high school came flooding back. When it came time for the concert, we all enjoyed singing with Mr. Lipke so much that we decided to form the North High Alumni Choir. Singing in the choir was great fun but a long distance to drive. So after 10 years, my wife talked me into quitting. It was costing too much for me to drive 36 miles one way to rehearsal every week.

Then, there's Pat . . .

I really missed being in a choir. A few years after I left the alumni choir, I saw an ad in the paper for auditions at a local choir. They rehearsed about 2 miles from home. Pat talked me into auditioning. I was scared crazy. I didn't know this choir or the director. I called a former choir friend, Vicki, for reassurance and she encouraged me to go ahead and audition. Surprisingly, the director said "I want you in my choir." So I began singing with this new choir, the South Metro Chorale. Sure, it was close to home. But then, the choir planned a concert tour to Europe. Not only did my wife encourage me to go, she signed up to come along. Hmmmm. Let me think about this. I quit the alumni choir to save gas money and I join another choir and end up taking a 10-day trip for 2 to Croatia? Where's my calculator . . .?

Finally, it's Suzanne . . .

So I'm in this new choir (the South Metro Chorale), now back from Croatia, and one of my choir mates (Suzanne) tells me I should join what's called the Oratorio Society's Summer Chorus. Why? Because, she says: "It'll be fun. There's no audition, it's only 6 rehearsals in July and you can ride with us (there are 2 other South Metro Chorale choir mates joining the Summer Chorus)." I talk to Pat about it. She's not excited about the prospect of me being gone 2 nights each week in July – the peak of summer. But, we had been to one Oratorio Society concert earlier that year and they are a really good choir – way better than any choir I'd ever sung with.

Suzanne persists and Pat eventually caves (certainly not because of anything I said).

The Summer Chorus was going to perform Mozart's *Requiem*, a work with which my only familiarity was from the movie "Amadeus." So I figured I should at least take a look at the music before the first rehearsal. I borrowed the score from someone in the choir and took a listen. OMG! This was going to be challenging. Thankfully, I had some time (it was still May). I practiced at every opportunity. And it's a good thing because when I got to the first rehearsal, the director started right off having us sing the first movement. I was shocked. Everyone already knew it. And it already sounded good!

Six rehearsals later, the 170-member chorus along with 30 musicians performed this amazing piece to an audience of about 700 people. From where I was sitting, it sounded fantastic. And the recording turned out very well. Pat enjoyed it, too.

I was so impressed with the director of the Oratorio Society's Summer Chorus (Matt Mehaffey) that I secretly arranged an audition for the regular season. I did it secretly because, if I wasn't accepted, no one would know and I wouldn't be embarrassed or ashamed about not getting in.

I arrived early for my audition and ended up having to wait in the parking lot. As I stood there on this sunny, warm, August afternoon, a car pulls in. At first I thought it was the director. Nope. It was another audition candidate. We got to talking and he told me he was a tenor from VocalEssense, a premiere Minneapolis choir. Damn, now I'm competing against the best of the best. I'll never get accepted.

So as soon as Dr. Mehaffey arrives he asks who wants to go first. I jump at the chance. I'm gonna get this over with and get the hell out of there. We go into his smallish office. There's a piano there along with his desk. I give him my music and he begins the audition. You gotta remember, auditioning is like taking a test - a test where your "answers" are judged

The Oratorio Society of Minnesota

immediately and in front of you. There's no escaping embarrassing mistakes. He goes through his routine - scales to determine range, sight reading, tonal memory and singing the song I brought along as my example. At the conclusion, he tells me I'm in! Wow! I actually made it into the Oratorio Society of Minnesota! I call Pat right away to tell her about it.

~   ~   ~

Four years later, I'm still singing in both choirs and the Oratorio Society has had sell-out performances. Some of us have even sung with Osmo Vänskä and the Minnesota Orchestra at Orchestra Hall in Minneapolis!

And if that weren't enough, several of us from the South Metro Chorale have sung with Shirley Jones in her "The Music Man in Concert" show. We were even paid to do it! Can you imagine?

~   ~   ~

Maybe listening to women pays off. But, one of these days I'm going to start making my own decisions.

Of course, the more likely scenario is that Pat will talk me into getting a dog!

Me and my grandfather's dog, Rex.

Busted!

This never happens:

Our daughter and son talking to each other.

Fighting, yes. Talking, never.

~   ~   ~

I'm having my usual breakfast at about 8:30 on a typical summer Saturday morning when our 17 year-old daughter, Tessa, comes downstairs. And she continues going to the lower level where our 21 year-old son's (Dan) bedroom is. I hear them talking.

Tessa

This seemingly minor, inconsequential event is odd in several ways:

1. Tessa never gets out of bed before 11.
2. Dan never gets out of bed before noon.
3. They never talk to each other.

As I said, this never happens.

After their conversation, Dan comes upstairs and announces he's going into town for a haircut. No big deal. When he returns, he goes to Tessa's room and they have another conversation! Hmmmm.

~ ~ ~

The remainder of the day continues without any additional surprises, odd behaviors or other unusual turns of events. Sometime during the afternoon Tessa tells us she's planning on going to a party that night - fairly typical of her Saturday night routine.

Evening arrives and it's time for our Saturday night movie. Pat and I always like to watch a movie on Saturday nights. Tonight's film is a spy thriller. One thing you need to know about me and movies is that I don't like being interrupted while watching. In fact, I don't like being interrupted so much that I will sometimes turn off the phone. I don't even like eating popcorn because it's too much of a distraction. Pat (my wife) knows this and will refrain from talking during movies. This is particularly important during a spy thriller, where you really have to pay close attention and observe every little, unspoken detail.

Dan and his cat, Tiger

~ ~ ~

So we're about 20 minutes into our movie. The phone is turned off and the suspense is building. Suddenly, Tessa goes outside with Dan. She returns after just a couple of minutes, goes back to her room and closes the door.

Alright, the suspense at home has now surpassed the suspense in the movie. I press the pause button on the VCR (remember VCRs?), tell Pat I'll be back in a minute and go upstairs to Tessa's room. I knock on her door.

She says *"Who is it?"*

"Dad"

"Come in."

64

I walk in and ask, *"Where's the beer?"*

Tessa says in a very surprised voice *"How did you know?"*

Busted!

She tells me the beer is in the trunk of Dan's car. I get Dan and together, the three of us walk to the car. I confiscate the 12-pack of her cheap beer. She says I owe her for it. I laugh.

Time to resume my movie.

The Inebriated Phlebotomist

I knew a guy once who made his own license plate tabs. He's dead now.

But that's not what killed him.

~   ~   ~

His name was Mike and he taught me everything I needed to know in my very first job out of college. I had been hired to work at Kallestad Labs, a small laboratory making an anti-rejection drug used by the University of Minnesota Hospitals for organ transplant recipients. It was called ALG (anti-lymphocyte gamma globulin). And Mike taught me numerous things about it [Warning: Science lesson ahead]:

- Mike taught me how to trim connective tissue off of human lymph nodes (a tedious job at best requiring hours of painstakingly cutting away the white-ish, thin layer of connective tissue from the lymph nodes).

- He taught me how to separate giant tubes of horse blood from the serum (a decidedly disgusting process involving blood clots nearly three feet long and several flushes of a nearby toilet).

Author's Note: No horses were harmed during the making of ALG.

- He taught me how to inject rabbits with samples of the drug for quality control testing. It required a steady hand, a sharp needle and a cooperative rabbit.

Another Author's Note: No rabbits were harmed either, although some did die unexpectedly. We were all very sad when this happened.

- And he taught me how to test the drug for potency.
- He also tried to teach me how to make my own license plate tabs, but I resisted.

After a few months of training, I became the best technician on staff (there were only seven of us), mainly because of my attention to detail and my propensity towards accuracy and precision.

Kallestad's operations were in an old dental office which, before that, had been someone's home. So it looked like anything but a laboratory, much less a dental office. The lab benches weren't stainless steel; they were white plastic laminate covered with burn marks from forgotten cigarettes. The walls weren't sterile white; they were a dirty yellow. And the floor wasn't shiny-clean linoleum; it was scruffy, old carpet. Even the walk-in cooler was just a wooden box pieced together and nailed to the side of the building. And you'd think that security in a place like this would be fairly stringent. Not. It was non-existent. Anyone could have walked in and stolen everything. Of course, what would they do with a 4-liter centrifuge, except maybe sell it to Iran?

Yet here we were, making this drug to be used by a world-renowned, prestigious organ transplant hospital by one of the world's most noted surgeons, Dr. John Najarian. If he only knew.

Oh, we were careful enough about our work. The quality was always above reproach and our record keeping very thorough. I made sure of it and so did our boss.

So it was in this environment, and in the spirit of actually doing something to help humankind (a little bit more meaningful than asking, "Would you like fries with that?") - that I really got committed and dedicated to this, my first job.

~   ~   ~

And I was good at it. So good that, whenever they needed to run a final quality control test, they'd ask me to do it. And this test involved some sacrifice. First, because its incubation took several hours, the test had to be started at 4:00 in the morning. And second, it required fresh, human blood. Really fresh. Like drawn within minutes of using it for the test. Now, I can't even pretend that I would draw my own blood for this test. And, because I couldn't draw it myself, it meant that someone else would also have to come to work at 4:00 in the morning. And that someone was always Mike (remember Mike?).

But here's the thing, Mike was young, enjoyed sometimes risky fun and loved to party. And when he partied, he especially liked to drink beer and smoke pot (see where this is going?)

On one occasion, Mike arrived right on time at 4:00 AM; and he was completely stoned. I don't even know how he was able to drive. Thankfully, I didn't think about that at the time.

He pulled out a fresh needle and said, "Are you ready, wild Bill?" "Sure", I said, trying as hard as possible not to think about his inebriated condition and avoiding any glances toward the teetering Mike or the wavering needle headed toward my unsuspecting arm. Mike stuck the needle in my arm and started to draw out some blood. He did it so effortlessly and smoothly I barely felt a thing. In fact, he's the best phlebotomist I've ever had!!!! I'll take him in his inebriated condition over some of the sober others who've drawn my blood any day.

~   ~   ~

Fast-forward more than a couple of years.

After church one Sunday morning, I was talking (you know how you have those brief, informal "Hi, how are you" conversations after church) with an acquaintance named Mary. She mentioned that she had had a kidney transplant several years earlier.

> *"Oh really?"* I said casually, pretending to be interested using my best Sunday conversation mode.

"I used to make a drug that was used to suppress the immune system of transplant recipients."

"Was it ALG?" she asked.

"Yes!" I said, now much more interested and no longer casual. I was surprised, no, shocked, that she knew what it was called.

Then she added how much she admired her doctor. She told me his name was Dr. Najarian, the same doctor to whom we sold ALG at the University of Minnesota when I worked at the lab.

Okay, so now this is getting a bit spooky. I had to ask the final question:

"Mary, when did you have your transplant?"

She answered, *"1971."*

Oh. My. God! That's the exact same time frame that I worked in the ALG department at Kallestad Labs. I was stunned.

I don't know what it meant for Mary. But for me, coming face to face with someone whose life was saved by a drug I helped to make was both humbling and gratifying.

~   ~   ~

I knew Mike a long time ago. He lived wild and died tragically young. Even so, his short life made a big difference to me, to Mary and who knows how many others.

And by the way, he never got caught for making his own license plate tabs.

Mr. Irrelevant

Our tour guide, Lana, said in her thick Croatian accent:

> *"This is not on the itinerary. I take no responsibility; you are on your own."*

The choral ensemble of which I am a member had just performed for a standing-room-only crowd in the ancient Church of St. Blaise in the old town section of Dubrovnik, Croatia. A well-dressed, elderly gentleman came forward to thank us for the concert. He was visibly moved by what he had just heard. In gratitude, he said (in broken English):

Church of St. Blaise

> *"I want to invite you all to my son's café for wine and cheese. It's just 400 meters down the road."*

Our tour guide was not pleased with this plan - she already had the bus ready to pick us up and return us to our hotel. "This is not part of the itinerary," she said. In the end, she said it was our decision and so, of course, we accepted the offer.

When we arrived at the café, it was so small there was barely enough room for all of us. But we squeezed in and were graciously served generous helpings of cheese, bread, prosciutto, wine and something called "Croatian medicine." Our host said the Croatian medicine "is good for the blood." It was a golden color, quite strong but entirely delightful, warming the throat as it went down.

We sang a couple of songs for our host and the woman minding the café. She got teary-eyed as we sang, presumably from joy and not because our singing was horrid (which I don't think it was).

As the evening progressed, our host, the well-dressed elderly gentleman, said that he had escaped during the Croatian War of Independence in the early 1990s from what was then Yugoslavia. He traveled to New York City where he married and made his fortune. After the fighting in Croatia ended in 1995, he returned to his home country. When we asked what his name was, he declined to tell us, saying:"It's irrelevant."

And that's how we remember him today - as Mr. Irrelevant.

Irrelevant or not, he sure made a lasting impression on all of us.

Mr. Irrelevant - elderly man on the right

Lost in London

London (England, that is) is big. I mean really big. Way bigger than Prior Lake, Minnesota (the town where I live) or even nearby Minneapolis and St. Paul put together. So big, you can get lost there. But I'm getting ahead of myself. Let me start from the beginning.

~ ~ ~

Our daughter, Tessa, was in London going to college as part of a semester abroad program. Having wanted to go to Europe since I was

her age, I was totally jealous. So when she came to us with the request of studying abroad, we agreed to help her get there financially. And going there as a student is much cheaper than as a tourist.

Tessa and friend Jamie doing the 'Abbey Road' pose.

So after a couple of months with Tessa in London, my wife, Pat, finds an incredible deal on airfare and buys two round trip tickets. We're going to visit London! I can't believe my good fortune. Not only do I get to go to Europe, I'll be visiting someone who actually knows something

73

about it, including how to navigate in that huge city. So there's no chance of me getting lost.

Our plane ride into Gatwick Airport (about 28 miles from London) is followed by a train trip into the city. As we leave Gatwick, we're surprised by the obvious presence of men in full military garb carrying assault rifles – a stark reminder of a post-9/11 world. I get to thinking that we are Americans in a city that strongly disapproves of the war in Iraq. George W. Bush is president and anti-American sentiment is strong in Europe. It's hard to hide the fact that we're Americans and I wonder if the Brits will somehow take their anger about U.S. foreign policy out on us.

We successfully get past the armed guards, buy our train tickets and get on board. The train ride into London is relatively unremarkable except that it was our first glimpse of the English countryside. And yup, it looks just like it does on TV - rectangular fields of green divided by stone fences, probably hundreds of years old. Very cool.

When our train arrives at the subway station (the tube, as they call it), we find the ticket booth and buy our tickets for the third leg of our journey - the tube ride to the hotel. One thing Londoners can do is buy a multi-use ticket called an Oyster. They load them up with money and can use them over and over again, much like our toll-road passes in this country. We opted out because we weren't planning on being in London that long.

Pat at the Canning Town Tube Station

After buying our tickets, we start jockeying through the throngs of people looking for directions to the subway (oops, I mean tube) that will take us to our hotel. The tube system is heavily used and never once did we find it not jam-packed with people. And they appear to be in a world all their own - as if they were the only ones on the train. So many people; and all alone! It seems as though they couldn't care less about anyone else, much less us Americans.

As we make our way through the station, I notice that we'll need our tickets to pass through a turn-style and go up the stairs to get to the correct tube platform. I slide my ticket into the turn-style, pull it out and pass through. My wife, Pat, is right behind me. She also swipes her ticket and tries to go through the turnstile but it won't budge. She tries again. No luck. Once more, and nothing. I'm standing on the other side, helpless to reach her. People are swarming all around us. What can I do? Ahhhhhhh! (silent scream).

Before I can even think about planning my move, a 30-something man walks up to Pat's turn-style, swipes his Oyster and walks on, not even looking back or using the turn-style. Pat's turn-style opens and she passes through without any further difficulty. The man who used his Oyster is long gone. Who was he? And why did he do that?

~   ~   ~

Navigating London is easy. The train system is a model of efficiency and ease of use. Everything is clearly marked. There are maps of the tube system everywhere and loud speakers announce trains as they arrive. On board, more loud speakers announce each stop as well as the train's final destination. It's impossible to make a mistake. They even tell you to "Mind the Gap" (the space between the train and the platform) when boarding.

We visit with Tessa for a couple of days touring Buckingham Palace, Westminster Abbey and the Tower of London. And she takes us to her favorite pub on a double-decker bus ride. I'm starting to feel right at home. Does it get any better than going to a pub for fish 'n' chips?

We then travel by train (departing from the famous Paddington Station) to the Cotswolds where we'll spend another couple of days touring the

English countryside in a town called Stow-on-the-Wold. It's smack in the middle of sheep country in the iconic, green-pastured landscape.

We stay in a bed & breakfast built in the 1640s and had a full English breakfast everyday. It was idyllic. Our host, Roger, recommended that we take time to also visit the next village, Bourton-on-the-Water. But we had so much fun just puttering around in Stow-on-the-Wold having "creamed tea," discovering a

Stow-on-the-Wold

centuries-old Roman water trough and testing a "kissing gate," that we ran out of time and didn't make it to Bourton-on-the-Water. Next day at breakfast, Roger asked if we were able to visit Bourton-on-the-Water. When he found out that we hadn't, he offered to take us there, if we had time. So we hopped in his car and he drove us to this charming village where he took a couple of photos of us standing next to the river that flows through town. What a nice gesture on Roger's part. He truly made our day!

Kissing Gate

Roman Spring

Pat and Bill at Bourton-on-the-Water

With our time in England almost over, we travel (again by train) back to London. From there, we'll need to get on a train that will take us back to Gatwick for our trip home. It's Sunday evening.

By now, I feel I've learned the "tube" system fairly well. I know what signs to look for, what announcements to pay attention to and how to get from one place to another. In short, I believe that, despite carrying luggage, I fit right in with all the other hundreds of people using the trains every day. I am now one of them. I am a seasoned and experienced train/tube traveler.

So when we arrive back in London, I look for a train that will take us to Gatwick. The sign tells us it's expected to arrive in 23 minutes. Guess we'll have to wait.

But hold on! There's another train arriving just now. That'll take us to Gatwick, I'm sure. We hop on, leaving the busy station in London behind.

As our train heads out of the city, I watch to make sure that we're passing towns that indicate where we are in relation to Gatwick. But something's not right. These aren't the towns I was expecting. I keep watching. At each stop, more and more people depart the train. Soon it's just us, a well-dressed guy several rows ahead of us and a young, leather-jacketed, scary-looking teenager with a boom box several rows behind us. I keep looking for towns with familiar names. I see none. It's getting later. On a Sunday night. Hardly anyone's around. And this train is headed into the dark unknown.

I desperately hate to admit it (being the perfectionist that I am) but I think we're lost. I confess my fear to Pat. Together we wonder what we can do. We decide I need to ask for help. Hmmm. Who should I ask? The well-dressed guy who looks like he's sleeping or the dangerous-looking teenager in the back? I think about my choices for a nanosecond and approach the guy up front. He jumps visibly in his seat as I say, "excuse me" (he <u>had</u> been sleeping).

> *"I think we're on the wrong train. Does this train go to Gatwick?"*

He stands up and together we look at the map, which is directly above his seat.

> *"I don't think so,"* he says.

> He adds, *"You can get off at Wimbledon and get the correct train there."*

I thank him and return with the news to Pat.

So now we watch for the Wimbledon stop and I get worried (and there's so much to worry about) that our tickets won't be good for the next train. We get off when we reach Wimbledon. Even though our train was nearly empty and it's really late on a Sunday night, there are hundreds of people there. Was there a tennis match the next day? Nah, probably not - it's November!

Anyway, I look for a train official and find one almost immediately. In England, they wear bright day-glow yellow vests and can be seen anywhere on a train platform. I show him our tickets and explain that we got on the wrong train. I told him we're trying to get to Gatwick. He explained what trains to get on, where to transfer and in what towns. It was all very confusing. None of the towns sounded familiar to me. I asked if he could write it down for me. He said "sure" and when he handed me the sheet of directions, he apologized for his handwriting and hoped I could read it. So helpful!

This man was a saint to us. He had saved us from taking another wrong train and got us to our Gatwick hotel without further complication.

In none of our encounters with the many British people we met did we feel any resentment or dislike because we were Americans. In fact, we felt quite the opposite, as if we were welcomed with open arms.

On this high note, our trip came to its conclusion. The Brits are the best!

Yoga and the Corpse

Birthdays come and go. More often than not, they pass without notice or fanfare outside the immediate family, except for when you reach a particular milestone. One of my recent birthdays was one of those that passed without fanfare. By the way, this lack of attention would be totally unacceptable if I were still a kid, which part of my brain still believes. But, that's another story.

So when my friend Suzanne invited me out to a birthday lunch (f.y.i. - several days after my special day!), I thought: "Sure, that would be nice," and we planned to meet up at a Mexican restaurant in Lakeville. It was a cold, dark and gloomy February day - typical of Minnesota in the winter.

The waiter took us to our table. Suzanne was carrying a few small packages - she had evidently been shopping - and she piled them on the table as we sat down. The waiter brought our waters and I started looking over the menu.

Suzanne then pulled out the contents of one of her packages. At first, I thought it was a birthday gift for me but it turned out to be a new type of panty hose she was excited about. Are you ready for this, because I wasn't! I think it was called "Spanx" and was, as she enthusiastically described it, designed to reduce tummy roll and hide panty lines! She needed them for her costume for the Cabaret fundraiser our choir would be putting on at the beginning of March. Okay, this is way more than I need to know about her wardrobe! Too much information!!!!!!

After we finished our meal, she brought out another of her shopping bags and handed it to me. To be honest, after the last one, I was a bit tentative about looking inside. But when I peeked in the bag, it appeared to be fairly benign. It was an envelope so I relaxed and assumed it was a birthday card. And, it was. But inside the card was something else - a gift card. I didn't recognize the card holder but when I pulled out the card and looked at the logo, I knew right away what it was. She had given me a gift card to a yoga center, the same one she frequents and has often talked about.

I was a little taken aback for a moment and couldn't think of what to say. What *was* this? Could it really be what I think it was - a gift card to a yoga studio? For me? Seriously? I looked at the back of the card - value $69!

Three thoughts immediately popped into my usually empty head:

 What a generous and thoughtful gift!

 What the heck am I going to do with it?

 I don't have a thing to wear!

I graciously thanked her and told her of my reluctance, hesitation and even trepidation about it. I have never stepped foot inside a yoga studio, know less than nothing about it and have never considered going to one. It's a girl's thing! The closest I've gotten to yoga is trying a couple of poses I saw illustrated in an AARP magazine. My favorite one was lying flat on the floor - a pose I can relate to and can do quite well, even if I do say so myself! As I learned later, it's aptly called the "Corpse Pose."

And so my birthday lunch concluded. I thanked Suzanne again and we went our separate ways. When I returned home, I placed the gift card on my desk where I wouldn't (or couldn't) forget about it and promptly determined I wouldn't have time to use it for several days, if not weeks. Procrastination is the best way of avoiding something you don't really want to do. But, putting it on my desk makes me completely innocent. You could say it has plausible deniability (I love that phrase). If she ever asked me about it, I could say, "Nope, I haven't forgotten about it. It's on my desk. I'm just waiting for when I have time to go."

Weeks pass. I've looked at the card almost every day. My time for plausible deniability is running out. She's bound to ask about it soon. I'll visit the yoga center's website to at least be able to say that I've checked into it. When I do, I discover that they offer a free 15-minute consultation. I make a call and schedule it for the next day. The woman is very pleasant albeit not really present. She continually looks away, seemingly to avoid eye contact. And when she does look in my direction, she doesn't really look *at* me. Perhaps she's bored. Perhaps I have bad breath. In any case, I get the full tour with some description of the services they offer and a couple of handouts. I don't schedule or commit to anything.

Let's face it. This is going to take a fair amount of courage. I have to think about what I'm going to wear and what I need to do when I go to my first class. I've resigned myself to going because, well, this was an expensive gift and I just can't blow it off. I even briefly consider giving it to my wife, Pat. I know she'd be more likely to use it than I would.

I put the card back on my desk.

The next week, I look at the center's handout and realize I may have some time later that week to attend my first session. I choose the "gentle" session, thinking it would be the easiest. I plan on going Thursday, in two days' time. I add it to my calendar - a key step in making anything happen. I send a Facebook message to Suzanne telling her what day I'm going. This way, she will know I'm using her gift, finally. She replies that she'll avoid going that day herself. She doesn't want me to feel intimidated.

I decide not to tell Pat of my plans. Doing anything at which I may fail carries risk and if I fail at something that no one knows about, it seems like less of a failure. Kind of like when you apply for a job (or audition for the Oratorio Society) but you don't want to tell anyone just in case you don't get it. Failure is embarrassing. Know what I mean?

Anyway, when Thursday arrives, I go to my first session. I've been told to wear comfortable clothes so I've decided to wear a t-shirt under my sweater and swim trunks under my pants - easy for changing into and out of. I've also been told that socks are not allowed. As it was explained to me: "We want our feet to be connected to the earth."

When I get there, I check in and the woman who avoids eye contact tells me I can change in the restroom. The instructor takes the yoga mat I borrowed from Pat (without her knowledge). After changing, I enter the classroom. There are probably 8 or 9 people in there, the lights are dimmed, ceiling fans gently move the air around and the window blinds are drawn so only a little daylight squeaks in. I find my mat, placed right in front near the instructor and the session begins.

The first thing the instructor, Jenn, says is "Close your eyes." Good, I think. I don't want anyone seeing me. Especially since I'm in the front row. She skillfully describes each pose. They get progressively more and more complex to the point where she has to address me by name saying, "Bill, do it this way," or something to that effect. There is evidently another male in the room because she calls instructions out to him, too. His name is Joe. While I can't see Joe, I can hear him because he's breathing heavily - almost like he's been running. The women in the class seem to know how to do everything because Jenn often praises them. "That's excellent, Josie," and, "Very good, Marlene," or "Beautiful pose, Sally." Obviously, she favors the women.

In the middle of the class, I suddenly realize how weird it is that we can't wear socks. We're supposed to be able to connect to the earth during yoga and wearing socks prevents that. Thing is, you're always on this plastic mat. So . . . . why can't I wear socks?

The "Never in Your Wildest Dreams" pose.

Not the author!

Some of the simplest poses are also the easiest to remember.

Among them are the Cow Pose, the Cat Pose and my all-time favorite, the Corpse Pose. I'm relieved when the session is over, and surprised that it ended so soon.

Even though I was able to do most of the poses, I didn't feel as though I connected with the process. My muscles were sore and I felt like this whole yoga thing was very foreign to me. Before leaving the room, Joe, the heavy breather, comes over to greet me. He wants to know what brought me here. I tell him a good friend gave me a gift certificate. He's very personable. But his pleasantness isn't enough for me to feel any better about doing yoga.

I changed my clothes and put on my shoes. As I got ready to leave, Jenn said something polite like "I look forward to seeing you again." I remember thinking "like that will ever happen" but said instead, "The time went really fast." How lame is that?

With this particular yoga studio, once you've had your first free session, you can attend as many times in the next week without charge. I went exactly zero times. In fact, I was doubtful I would ever go again. I decided yoga was not my thing.

A week passes. I have another Thursday morning free. It's raining outside so I decide to go to another session. I even mention it to Pat this time telling her I didn't feel the first session went very well. She said maybe I should give the card back to Suzanne. I disagreed. That would be rude. I think she was using reverse psychology and just trying to get me to back off giving up on the idea.

When I check in at the desk, the woman who doesn't make eye contact asks how I'd like to pay. I give her my gift card, she swipes it and surprises me by not giving it back. What the heck? Then, she adds that I'll have 30 days to use the unlimited visits my card purchased. In some odd way, I feel relieved that she didn't give the card back. Like the pressure for following through with more visits is gone because I no longer have to look at the card sitting on my desk.

There are fewer people in class today and Joe, the guy from the first class, isn't there. Jenn gives her same, kind and patient instruction every time I mess up. At one point, I thought it was over and started getting up to leave when she continued with more poses. Oops! Another opportunity for me to feel stupid.

When the class is truly over, I thank Jenn and leave the classroom to go put on my socks thinking I should really ask someone about the feet connecting to the earth through a plastic mat issue. This could be yoga's fatal flaw!

As I began putting on my coat my gaze falls on someone I wasn't expecting to see there. It was Suzanne! She had also just put on her coat. I assumed she had gone to the another session held in a different room. I asked if she wanted to go out for a coffee. When we sat down at the coffee shop and started talking about yoga, she repeated things that Jenn had said during my class. Suddenly, a terrifying possibility dawned on me. I asked: "Were you in the same class as me?" "Yes," she said. I was shocked. I had no idea. She must have been on the opposite end of the classroom. I asked her if she knew it was me that Jenn had addressed during the class. She said she suspected it was. Shit. How embarrassing. Failure exposed!

I can't wait to see what birthday gift she surprises me with next year. On second thought, maybe I can.

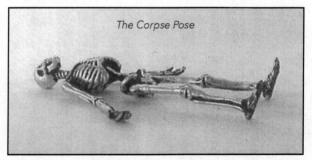

The Corpse Pose

This is one pose the author can do although he's not pictured here.

A History of Hair - The Long and the Short of It

We're in Rod Janowski's college dorm room, May 1967. Janowksi is there, along with the other guys Ganske, Schleck, Heebink, DuBrow, and me. It's hot. The sun is pouring in. Everyone is sweating. Janowski is standing behind me, holding a loaded . . . pair of scissors!

˜   ˜   ˜

I've always been a little self-conscious about my hair. Just ask my wife. I take pride in the way it looks, although aging hasn't done anything favorable to enhance its appearance.

When I was growing up in Massachusetts, my parents had control over my hair. They kept it really short – a buzz job. Back in Massachusetts, we called that kind of haircut a "heinie." When I had to go for a haircut, they'd just tell the barber, "Give him a heinie." It wasn't until I prepared this story that I figured out why they called it a "heinie." Think about it.

When I was 12, we moved to Minnesota and my parents allowed my hair to grow a bit - long enough to comb. And when I got to junior high, it grew a bit more, although not enough to do the Elvis Presley look. You might remember his greasy, ducktail look with the sides slicked back. I never liked Elvis or his special hair. But just to show I was cool, I did use lots of Brylcreem (even though "a little dab'll do ya"). And because I was

Remember
Dick Clark?

trying to be so cool, I kept it neatly combed all the time. Somehow, I sensed that, along with my dark brown "cow" eyes (as my neighbor Linda Fredrickson always called them) it was my best feature. Linda was a couple of years younger than me and very cute. We used to play kissing games after dark with the other kids in the neighborhood. I was flattered that she thought my eyes looked like cow eyes. After she grew up, she became a nun. I always wondered if my kissing was the reason.

But even though Linda liked my cow eyes (and by my own extension, my hair), I was often teased and sometimes bullied in junior high by the tough guys that wore their hair in ducktails and dressed and walked like Elvis. Sometimes they would just mock me by calling me names like pansy-waist. Other times they'd smack the back of my head while I sat quietly in class. And when I told Mr. Joy (our teacher) about their abuse, he just said: "Oh, they would never do that!" After a while, I gave up complaining and just avoided them whenever possible.

~   ~   ~

Janowski (whose steaming-hot dorm room we started out in) was a tough guy, too. He lived on the same floor in the dorm I'd moved into during my sophomore year of college. He came from Chicago and drove a flashy, red Corvette. He struck me as being a spoiled little brat who thought pretty highly of himself – kinda like those junior high bullies. And he had real short hair. I didn't choose to hang out with him. In fact, I could have easily avoided him. But he was already part of the group of guys I hung out with so I was forced to accept being around him. It was during my college years that I started letting my hair grow longer. Hey, it was the 60s, I didn't live at home, freedom of expression came of age and the girls seemed to like it.

College also provided me with some courage. I was on my own and doing okay. I didn't need mom and dad to manage my hair anymore. I was becoming my own person. No more would I have to put up with school principals who yelled at you for overdue library books. No more would I have to sit quietly in class while bullies like Rod Janowski whacked the back of my head. No more would kids call me embarrassing names. I was free! And I could wear my hair however I wanted.

~   ~   ~

So it's May 1967 and we're all in Janowski's room. It's late afternoon, the sun is streaming in and it's hot, really hot. Janowski has something playing on his stereo, the Rolling Stones maybe. I'm looking at the album cover jacket and we're just hanging out. Now besides being an arrogant jerk, Janowski has this thing about his record albums. He's one of those people who doesn't ever take the protective plastic off. You slice the plastic open on the end and slide the LP out ever so carefully so as not to scratch the record or mar the album cover. I know how he feels about it because I used to do exactly the same thing. Heck, I might even have records with the plastic still intact today.

Anyway, we're sitting around in his sweltering room and Janowski starts mocking me about my hair. I think he says I need to get it cut. I brush off his remarks (pun intended). He's just being a tough guy again. But then he opens his desk drawer and pulls out a scissors and threatens that he's gonna cut it for me.

"The hell you will," I say. "Wanna bet," he counters. And in the most bold and confident manner I can muster I say, "I dare you."

He says, "Gurnon, you need a haircut and I'm gonna give it to you." And he stands up and walks toward me, scissors in hand. He steps behind me. I'm still holding his LP jacket.

He says: "Here goes."

I say: "You cut one single hair on my head and I swear I'll rip the plastic right off this album."

The room becomes totally silent. Nobody moves. Nobody says a word. Nobody dares breathe. I don't even hear the music anymore. All eyes are on Janowski and me. It's like the clock has stopped. Everyone waits for something to happen. It's a standoff; a shootout. Picture Blondie, Tuco and Angel

Eyes in that famous standoff walking the open circle in a cemetery from the movie *The Good, The Bad and The Ugly*.

The standoff seems to go on forever.

I wait.

We all wait.

Will he do it . . . ?

Then, I hear Janowski cocking his scissors. He grabs a lock of my hair and - - - SNIP!

Immediately and without hesitation, I vigorously rip the plastic wrap off his LP cover with as much vengeance and drama as I can muster.

The guys gasp. The room falls silent again. I wait for Janowski's reaction.

Nothing happens. He doesn't cut any more hair. He just walks back to his chair and sits down.

And that's the end of it.

He never teased me again. And I was never reluctant to be around him again. In a way, I think we became friends after that.

Maybe the longer hair gave me strength; like Samson?

Nah!

~   ~   ~

Forty-seven years later, things haven't changed much.

It's 2014 and I'm at my 50th high school reunion. I was hesitant about going. Except for a few special friends, I haven't kept in touch with those from my high school years. But I'd already paid for our tickets and so decided to go.

The place was packed. There were over 100 people in the room and it was hot. Not as hot as Janowski's room on that tense day 47 years earlier, but still hot. We'd had dinner and I was getting bored. You can sit through viewing 50-year old high school photos and inane blabber only so long before it's time to get on with your real life.

Anyway, the emcee was announcing all these silly awards like who came the farthest and who had the most great-grand kids and who'd been married to the same person the longest. The best one was who had the most body parts replaced! Good grief! This is getting way too old-ish for me. I gotta get outta here!

Each winner received a bottle of wine.

Then came the next award. Are you ready for this?

"The male with the most hair on his head!"

Guess who won.

Grand Marais Good-bye

Can a lake prevent a car from starting?

On our first trip to Grand Marais, MN our family fell in love with Lake Superior and the town. I was especially smitten with Artist's Point - the waves, the rocks and the sweet smell of lichens and moss all over everything.

But after only three days there, it was time to head home. We packed up the car, loaded the kids and started out. As we headed up the small hill in town, I could see the lake in the rear view mirror. That's when the car stalled. Try as I might, it wouldn't start again. It was a foggy morning so I thought maybe there was some moisture in the fuel line. I bought some "Heat" gas line treatment and tried starting the car again. Still nothing.

Finally my wife, Pat, said to me, "Bill, it's time to let the Lake go. We'll be back, I promise." I took a deep breath, looked back at the lake, and tried starting the car again. This time it went. And we've been back to Grand Marais every year since.

Author's Note: *A 60-second video version of this story appeared on the local PBS station (tpt2) in the Twin Cities. The video was created as part of the Legacy Letters project produced by Envision Minnesota and tpt2. The Legacy Letters series won an Emmy Award in 2010. To view the video, visit:*

http://www.gurnon.com/Samples.html]

The Day the Peanut Butter Went Missing

When the children were younger, I was responsible for keeping the house stocked with all essential groceries like milk, toilet paper and peanut butter. As all good parents know, peanut butter is a relatively healthy food that's great in kids' lunchbox sandwiches. And besides, they like it. So it's important to always have a jar on hand.

On this particular day, when I went to the pantry for something else, I noticed the peanut butter jar was gone. I scrounged around on the shelf but couldn't find it. I looked on all the other shelves and still couldn't find it. This is serious. Every good and respectable household needs peanut butter. I'd better get to the store ASAP to get some more. But first . . . .

~   ~   ~

Our kids were old enough to have a history of eating snacks in their rooms. I'll bet one of them has taken the peanut butter there and failed to return it. Failing to return anything to its proper place in our house is an offense punishable by the loss of something really important, like the use of the item in question for a full day. Or at the very least, punishable via a stern reprimand in the most disapproving voice I can muster. I resolve to search all bedrooms until the peanut butter is found. But I'll have to wait until the juvenile delinquents have gone to school.

So once everyone has left the house, I begin my search. First, to the most likely kid's room, the oldest teenager, also known as the one who cleans up the least. In short, he's a slob.

I carefully open the door to his room. I'm clearly entering forbidden and dangerous territory. The room is a disaster. Homework papers, empty chip bags and Mountain Dew cans everywhere. The floor is so covered with stuff I can't even find a place to step without crunching on something. I don't even want to look through this mess but I'm sure the peanut butter is here somewhere. So I start gingerly picking up things and moving things to see if the missing jar is anywhere under this stuff. I look on his desk, on his headboard and on the bookshelf. No peanut butter. It must be here; I just can't see it. I resolve to come back later and look again.

But next to another room – the daughter's. She's less of a snack-aholic but her room is also a disaster. I pick through her stuff, look in all the places one might put a jar of peanut butter (under the bed, in the closet) but come up empty handed.

On to the next room.

Our youngest son is also a teenager and also a messy room keeper. I'm starting to see a pattern here. Are we bad or ineffective parents? I search through his junk but find nothing.

Again, I check the oldest son's room but still turn up nothing. With firm conviction that all our kids are inconsiderate slobs, I give up the search.

Several hours later, I'm in the kitchen again, this time preparing our evening meal. The kids are home and we're waiting for my wife to arrive from work. As I prepare the meal, I need to find an item from the pantry and as I have the door open, I glance at the door shelves and see the long lost peanut butter, right where I'd left it the day before.

Ooops!

Is that Katie over There?

Is that Katie over there?

It's August and my wife and I are in our son's school gymnasium watching a presentation (I think they called it a "pep fest") for new senior high students. Our son would be entering the 9th grade next month and the school wanted to instill some school spirit in these students new to this more grown-up school experience.

So we're sitting there on the typically uncomfortable gym bleachers with hundreds of other parents listening to the speeches and watching the cheerleaders dance around as the band played the school song. Our son wasn't terribly impressed with the whole thing and I must confess, neither was I. To combat boredom, I started to scan the room for people I might know. After all, we've lived in this community for nearly 20 years; surely there would be someone else there I knew and could wave to.

That's when I spotted her - a girl that looked a lot like our daughter's best friend, Katie. She had the same color blonde hair, wore it the same way Katie does in a big braid down her back, and was about Katie's height. But she was in the crowd of high school kids sitting on the gym floor, quite a distance from us way up in the bleachers, so I couldn't be sure it was she. The strange thing about it is that I thought Katie was driving up north with our daughter, Tessa.

~   ~   ~

Some days earlier our daughter, Tessa (a soon-to-be senior in high school) who was about 17 years old, asked if she could have permission to go to her friend's cabin in northern Minnesota for a few days. Remember, it's August in Minnesota and it's hot so this request is not so unusual.

So, like the very good parents we are, we started asking questions:

- Where is it?
- What lake is it on?
- Will there be grown-ups there?
- How long will you be gone?
- Who's driving?
- Who else is going, or more specifically, will there be boys there?

All of these are reasonable questions, right? We thought so too, and Tessa didn't put up the usual fuss about answering them.

Her plan was to leave the same day as the pep fest we were now attending with our son, Alex.

Now, I don't remember the details of Tessa's other answers and it's mostly unimportant anyway. But what I do remember is:

1. There would be no boys there.
2. They were going to Samantha's cabin, and
3. Katie (remember Katie, the blonde who we thought we saw in the high school gymnasium?) was going to be the one driving.

So here's the big question. If Katie and Tessa were driving up north to someone's family cabin, why am I looking at Katie now in the high school gymnasium?

I turn to my wife, Pat, and ask if she thinks that's Katie over there? She says, "How can it be? Tessa's driving up north with her. But it does look a lot like Katie."

Hmmmmm. What now?

At this point, I leave the gymnasium and call Tessa's cell phone. There's no answer so I leave a message. It went something like this:

> "Hi, Tessa. Who are you driving up north with? We saw
> Katie at the high school tonight."

When Pat and I got home, there was a message on the home phone. It's from Tessa:

> "Hi Mom and Dad. I'm not driving with Katie. I'm
> driving with Brian."

Immediately, I call her back. She asks if she's in trouble. I don't answer. I want to know exactly where she's going and why she lied. Turns out she's going to someone else's cabin, that there will be boys there, but adults will also be present, so we shouldn't worry. I told her that I needed to hear from an adult as soon as she arrived there.

So it wasn't too much longer that we did get a call from Brian's mother. I told her about Tessa's deception and let her know that I was angry about it. She said they would keep a close eye on the kids. I reminded her that Tessa was a minor and was there without parental approval. I asked that she be driven home that same day. The woman (Brian's mom) objected saying that there's no reason to punish Brian since he knew nothing of the deception. And she assured me that Tessa would be okay. Then, she put Tessa on the phone.

Tessa made no objection to being in trouble and asked what her consequence would be. (We always used "consequences" on the kids, rather than "punishments." Somehow it seemed more humane.) I told her I didn't know yet. I wanted her to sweat it out and *NOT* enjoy her weekend!

When she arrived home after the weekend, she came right to my office asking about her consequence. I told her, "One week of being grounded." She didn't argue. It was probably a bit lenient, but I had cooled down by then. Nothing had happened except that she lied. In the end, she turned out to be a good kid anyway.

Cats, Coyotes and Close Calls

There's a coyote pack that regularly roams our neighborhood looking for food. We hear the pack howling at night but have never seen it, except for one of its members - we call him Bob. Bob visits our property regularly during daylight hours so, not only have we seen him, I've been able to capture a few photos of him.

Coyotes are omnivores which means they'll eat most anything. Bob often finds rodents and wild turkeys to eat and when he gets really hungry, he'll eat the cob corn I put out for the deer.

Coyote 'Bob' inspecting a rodent he'd just caught.

~   ~   ~

We have two cats living with us, Peanut and his step sister, Juno. Both are mostly indoor cats. I say "mostly" because they are allowed outside but only with adult supervision, usually for less than an hour, depending on the weather and how much time we're willing to give to the effort. We don't let them stay outside partly because we know

Coyote Bob would eat them.

We've had outside cats prior to Peanut and Juno but they tended to collect dead things and bring them to the back door. Sometimes they even dismantled the dead things looking for something inside, although I'm not at all certain what it might be. And in the process of dismantling these dead things, they occasionally collected living things – parasites mostly. Then, when the cats brought their little, living-thing prizes into the house, we'd all get to enjoy the benefits of multiple living things crawling in our beds. So, in addition to our fear of a hungry coyote, our current cats, Peanut and Juno, are not allowed outside except, as I've said, with adult supervision.

~   ~   ~

Now this story takes place in the winter in Minnesota, so you might be able to deduce that it's cold outside and not very likely that we'd be taking our cats out for supervised playtime anytime soon. It's just not gonna happen.

But on one particular night in December, something happened. I was at choir rehearsal and not at home. My wife, Pat, was also not at home until about 9:00 PM and it was then that she decided to hang a holiday wreath outside on the front door. Being in the dead of winter, it was quite dark outside when she did this. When I got home about midnight, Pat was already sleeping and I slipped quietly into our bed unnoticed. I was apparently also unnoticed by the cats, as there were no cats to greet me when I came into the house. But, at that hour, I didn't really expect there would be any greeting anyway.

Next morning, after we'd had our coffee and sat down to breakfast, we realized we hadn't seen Peanut yet. He usually visits us as we're having our morning coffee. We called. Nothing. We checked his bed. He wasn't there. We called again. Again nothing. Hmmmm.

So we launched a whole-house search, looking in closets, nooks and crannies in the basement, even in rooms that are closed to keep the cats out. He's nowhere to be found. By now it's 7:30 AM and the sun is coming up. We start calling outside – Pat out the back door, me out the front. Still nothing. Pat starts to get worried, even a little teary-eyed.

You see, Peanut is the best possible cat we've ever had. He's loaded with spunk and personality and he loves to talk. That's what he does while we have our morning coffee. He'll trot upstairs talking all the way. He'll come into our room, still talking, looking for a good chin rub. After a few minutes of more talking and more chin rubbing, he's off to watch for squirrels and birds out the dining room window. This is his daily routine. It never varies.

So it's really odd that he wouldn't show up for his morning routine. Could he be sick somewhere? Could he be somewhere in the house we haven't looked yet? Or, could he have slipped out of the house unnoticed as Pat hung the wreath the previous night? We are clueless and totally immersed in finding him. At this moment, nothing could be more important.

We continue calling, louder now, out both the front and back doors. Finally, Pat sees him trotting up toward the house from behind the shed in the backyard. He comes in, gets a bite to eat and lies down in the sun – all as if nothing's happened. Pat weeps for joy. We give him a quick once over, which annoys him. He looks okay except that his paws are bright red, not the usual pink. Thankfully, it didn't get too cold overnight – about 25 degrees. He must have walked around the house all night long checking the doors for any signs of his family missing him. Poor little guy.

Peanut

The next night, the coyote pack (Bob and his friends) that frequents our neighborhood came through the yard yipping and howling, and looking for a meal. Close call for Peanut!

Nowadays, we do a tail count each night before we go to bed. It's the only way to be sure Peanut doesn't escape unnoticed.

WCAL: Real Radio, Real People

WCAL wasn't just America's _first_ listener-supported radio station, it was the _friendliest_.

~   ~   ~

When I found St. Olaf's WCAL, I really connected to the warm, neighborly style of its program hosts. Listening was like having a cup of coffee with them. They seemed so friendly. I wanted to get to know them better. I wanted to work

there. But when I asked about jobs, there were no openings.

But wait. No openings? No problem. I'll volunteer! When the next pledge drive started, I signed up to answer phones. And, guess what? I got to meet those convivial program hosts. And, they were just as friendly in person as on the radio.

Every six months I'd volunteer again and re-connect with my radio friends. It was great fun. They made me feel like part of the family. It was almost as good as working there.

WCAL is gone, but I'll always remember those friendly voices.

[Note: A video version of this 60-second story appeared on the local PBS station (tpt2) in the Twin Cities as part of the 2011 _Legacy Letters_ series produced by Envision Minnesota and tpt2. To view it, visit:

http://www.gurnon.com/Samples.html]

A Visit with the Chickens

<u>Question</u>: What do you get when you visit a friend's home for pie and a movie?

<u>Answer</u>: *Campylobacter* (a bacterium that sometimes causes abortion in animals and food poisoning in humans).

~   ~   ~

My wife (Pat) makes the best pies I've ever tasted and so I like to share them with friends. It was in this spirit of sharing a "best pie" experience that we visited Suzanne and David's home one September Saturday evening, bringing along one of Pat's freshly baked apple pies. As we arrived, we exchanged the usual pleasantries, greeted the dogs and went into the backyard where we visited their chickens.

Now, when you're at Suzanne and David's visiting the chickens, you don't just have a quick look, and then go back into the house. Oh, no. You must hold them. Suzanne makes sure everyone gets a chicken to hold. Have you ever held a chicken? It's actually quite interesting. They snuggle right into you and make this kind of cooing sound, which gets more frequent and louder if you stroke their tiny heads. Chickens are surprisingly soft, except for their feet, which feel like pinecones except that they are also

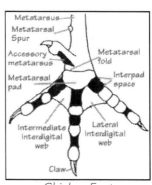

Chicken Foot
(Univ. of Illinois Extension)

unexpectedly very warm – almost hot. They're designed for scratching the ground as they search for food.

To actually hold a chicken, you place one hand under its feet and the other around the body. The chicken will just sit there cooing in your hand, quite content as you stroke it. As we hold the cooing birds, Suzanne cautions us to keep our feet-supporting hands away from the chicken's bottom so as to avoid an unpleasant surprise.

After a polite amount of time getting to know the chickens (mine had rich, reddish feathers, by the way), we went inside, sat down and had some pie. It was still warm and very delicious. After eating, we watched a movie, visited a bit more and went home. I think it's safe to say a good time was had by all.

~   ~   ~

Two Days Later . . .

It is now Monday evening and I've arrived home about 10 PM after choir rehearsal. Since it's bedtime, I climb under the covers and settle in. And almost immediately, I feel an unexpected chill, one that actually makes me shiver. I'm surprised (it is September so it's not cold outside) but fall asleep with no further ado.

The next morning, I wake up really sick (ah, that's what the shivering was all about). I rarely get sick because I take relatively good care of myself being certain to eat sort of okay, take vitamins and supplements, exercise regularly and, most importantly, perform a frequent hand-washing routine to avoid other people's germs. When I do get sick, it's done and gone in a day or so. Knowing this about myself, I never get flu shots – waste of time and money. So with all this in mind, I figure that I'll be feeling better by Wednesday. I also decide to skip my Tuesday choir rehearsal so as not to infect others.

Wednesday comes and I'm not better yet. What's up with that? After a small breakfast, I climb back into bed thinking that all I need to do is rest up a bit. Thursday will be better.

Wrong! Thursday is no better. Neither is Friday, Saturday or Sunday. I must have the flu. Maybe I should have gotten a flu shot after all.

By Monday (now over a week since I first fell ill), I decide to set up a doctor's appointment. At the doctor's office, they collect blood and other (unmentionable) specimens for laboratory analysis. The doctor also gives me a prescription for an antibiotic, in case it turns out to be an infection. She said that, if I decide to fill it, I'll start feeling better by the next day. Since she gave me the option, I decide to wait. In addition to not wanting to take flu shots, I don't like taking prescription drugs. The body should be able to heal itself, right?

Two days later, the doctor calls me and says I have a bacterial infection and that, if I haven't already, I should begin taking the antibiotic immediately. Then she asks a few very detailed questions about my eating habits.

1. Have I eaten any under-cooked meats or fish lately?
2. Any raw foods?
3. Had I been in contact with bird feces?

I immediately think of the wild turkeys that travel through our yard daily and how my cat, Peanut, is often walking around the same yard, probably stepping on turkey poop. Maybe that's it.

But then it hits me. It wasn't the wild turkeys. Why should I blame them? It was Suzanne's red-feathered chicken with the hot feet. And I realized that I had neglected to wash my hands after holding that blankety-blank chicken and before having pie at her house.

I really don't think I licked my fingers but somehow, I had infected myself.

I took the antibiotic but it required a second, stronger prescription to knock the infection out of my system. All in all, I was sick for about a month.

End of story? Nope.

~   ~   ~

A few days after my diagnosis, I get a call from the State of Minnesota Department of Health. The caller identified himself and asked if I had time for a few questions. The questioning lasted 20 minutes and included such questions as:

1. Where do I shop for meat and vegetables?
2. What brands do I buy?
3. Do we cook the meat and fish properly?
4. And finally, where do I think I got the infection?

I tell him about my brief encounter with Suzanne's chicken and how I failed to wash my hands afterward. He wanted to know where she lived. I told him in the southern suburbs.

"Where?"

"Dakota County"

"What city?"

"Burnsville"

I feared that he'd want to know specific details about Suzanne and where she housed her chickens.

Thankfully, he didn't press the issue any further.

Moral of the story: Don't hold Suzanne's chickens!

You're Such a Tart!

When your wife tells you she doesn't want any more jewelry for her birthday, this is good news!

~   ~   ~

When you've been married for nearly 30 years, it can be a challenge choosing that perfect birthday gift. The challenge is magnified when the woman to whom you're married tells you that she doesn't want any more pictures of flowers to hang on the wall and already has enough jewelry. Hard to believe that any woman would ever have enough jewelry but that's what she said!

What's a guy who desperately wants, once again, to totally impress his wife with the most wonderful and romantic gift ever, to do?

One week before her birthday, I still haven't figured this out. It's a Tuesday night, just after choir rehearsal when a few of us are out replenishing our fluids and moisturizing our dry throats at the local Axel's Bonfire. Now this group isn't aware of my somewhat scary/ frustrating kitchen adventures so when they ask what kind of cake am I baking for my wife's birthday, I just tell them I'll probably go to the DQ and pick up an ice cream cake.

The response was unanimous: "Ewwwwww."

Hmmmm. Maybe this isn't such a good idea.

Then, without hesitation, my friend Suzanne said she had a really good recipe for a lime tart. She instantly has my attention. As it happens, one of my wife Pat's favorite foods is key lime pie so I'm thinking she might like this. Not only that, but Suzanne volunteers to make it for me!

Okay, so having Suzanne make Pat's birthday cake is going a bit too far, don't you think? Then, I have an idea. I could go to Suzanne's house and help her make it. When I pitch this idea to Suzanne she says: "Better yet, you come to my house and I'll *teach* <u>you</u> how to make it."

Deal. Now I just have to figure out how I'm going to sneak out of the house on a Saturday afternoon to make the tart.

The weekend quickly approaches and I still haven't come up with a good reason to be gone from the house. You see, when weekends arrive, we tend to plan everything around what each of us must do. For example, if I must cut the grass we'll plan our usual grocery shopping trip so that it doesn't conflict with the 3-hour lawn project. Then it dawns on me. I can use my son as an excuse.

So I tell Pat that I need to go shopping with Alex (our son) Saturday afternoon so that he can pick out her birthday gift (I know this sounds pretty flimsy but hey, can you come up with something better?).

Meanwhile, Suzanne gives me an ingredients list. I'm all set. I've stated, in advance, my plans to be gone Saturday afternoon, have my list of ingredients and feel really good about this surprise gift.

Saturday arrives. I say goodbye to Pat and leave for Suzanne's, with a stop at the grocery store along the way to pick up the necessary ingredients.

When I arrive at Suzanne's, she immediately goes into teaching mode, telling me exactly everything I need to do - and she makes me do all of it, as she watches. She teaches me how to break open an egg and separate the yolk from the white. She teaches me how to grind up the cookies which will be used as the crust. And she teaches me how to beat all the ingredients together, spread the cookie crust, bake it, add the mixed filling, and so on. And while we're doing all this, Suzanne's husband, David, is videotaping the entire process. Who knows why. Maybe he's going to post it on Facebook.

Anyway, the final product finishes baking and is cooling down. Suzanne grabs a Victoria's Secret bag so that I have something with which to carry the lime tart. It's actually a pretty good idea since when I hand the bag to Pat, she'll think I went shopping for her gift there.

But as I begin to leave Suzanne's, my cell phone rings. It's Pat.

"Where are you?" she says.

"Shopping," I reply.

"Is Alex with you?"

"No, he called and said he didn't feel well."

"So, you've been shopping this whole time?"

"Yes."

"When are you coming home?"

"I'm on my way now. See you soon."

When I arrive home, she immediately starts questioning me. She asks why I was gone so long, where was I, and so on. But, lying is no longer needed and I hand her the Victoria's Secret bag. She looks inside and can't believe what she sees. I tell her it's a lime tart. She almost cries when I tell her I made it myself.

Score!

Just One Thing To Do

I had just one thing to do.

It was to be my son's high school graduation open house and I had to pick up the draft root beer from the liquor store.

This would become one of my life's many adventures with root beer. And, I'm here to tell you, not all of them were pleasant.

~   ~   ~

My first memory of root beer was when I was growing up in Massachusetts. Our neighbor across the street made it - from scratch. She was the crabby mother of two kids, a boy and a girl, about my own age somewhere around 9 or 10 years old. The only thing we did together was wait for the school bus which stopped right by the telephone pole at the end of my driveway. She dressed her kids in the oddest clothes. The girl wore dingy little dresses and the boy wore shorts (long before I ever saw boys wearing shorts) and shoes with a strap - like what you'd see on a girl. And even though they were neighbors, our families never did anything together and I never played with either of the kids - except for those times she invited me to have some homemade root beer. As I said, she made it from scratch. From my young perspective, it was her only redeeming quality. I always wondered where she got the roots.

~   ~   ~

Root beer played a somewhat limited role in my life for many years after this. Oh sure, there was that one time that my grandmother in

Minnesota bought root beer "Fizzies," a soda tablet. She'd plop one into a glass of water for instant draft root beer. But, between you and me, it just wasn't the same. Fizzies never really caught on. And, I'd bet you've never even heard of them although, surprisingly, you can still buy them. I found a website for them just the other day!

~   ~   ~

Still more years followed until the time my son Alex was about to graduate from high school.

Alex's high school graduation was on the household calendar and my wife (Pat) was heavy into planning the open house to celebrate his accomplishment. We had gone through the list of family and friends we wanted to be there and sent out the invitations, complete with the obligatory graduation photo.

About two weeks before the date of the open house, my wife was making a list of food and beverages she thought we should serve to our guests. We wanted to keep it simple with minimal use of dishes (less cleaning up

Alex

for me to do, right?) so we ordered subs and pizza from Davanni's. Easy to prepare and easy to clean up afterwards.

What about beverages? Hmmm. I suppose some kind of soft drink like lemonade for the kids and coffee for the adults. But wait, Pat has another idea. And this time, I actually agree with her. It's a great idea – draft root beer. We'd had some at a party recently. Alex loves root beer and so do the adults I know, including me. A friend told me that you can get it at any liquor store. Excellent, we have a plan. And, since this was a liquor store item, Pat asked me if I could make the arrangements. Sure, no problem. I can handle this one thing.

~   ~   ~

So I made a trip to the liquor store to find out how to go about getting some of this draft root beer. And I find out it's really easy. I'm glad to help with this piece of the open house and I'm especially pleased that it's so easy. All I have to do is order it a week in advance and pick it up the day of the party. Almost too easy . . . .

~   ~   ~

The big day arrives. I've cleaned the bathrooms (something else I can do that keeps me out of the kitchen) and now it's time for me to pick up the root beer - my one thing to do. Because it is truly draft root beer, it comes in a keg. Not like a big beer keg that I know you're picturing. It's smaller. It will sit nicely on the kitchen counter. The clerk at the liquor store explains how to dispense the root beer. He says it's really easy and points to the dispenser on the container.

"*See,*" he says.

"*Just follow the instructions.*"

"**Push, pour and enjoy.**"

Wow, that is easy. I can handle this.

So I pay for it, take it home and set it up on the counter. And I decide to test it, to make sure it tastes okay. And it does. It's delicious. Great. My one job is finished. Time to relax.

Our guests begin arriving and one of the first things I do is offer them a glass of real draft root beer. They're all clamoring to get some. So, following the instructions, I begin to push and pour so that they can enjoy. About a half a glass comes out, and nothing more. What the heck! The container is full and nothing comes out? What up with that? Try again. Nothing. As you might expect, others (the men) elbow their way to the keg. "Here, let me try," they say. But they can't do it either. Nothing will come out and I have thirsty guests waiting for something I can't provide.

A friend, Pegi, saw that I was getting frustrated and upset and she decided to take over. She called the liquor store and explained the problem. Pegi can be very persuasive and insistent and before I knew it, she had talked the guy at the liquor store into delivering another mini-keg of root beer. To the best of my recollection, she explained it this way. "The party is well under way and you need to get the root beer over here right now!" And he did! Except this time, he brought a full-sized keg. Thank you, Pegi!

It worked beautifully. We drank root beer until we could hold no more. We were giving it away, in any container we could find, to people as they left the party and still we had plenty left over – gallons of it. It sat in the refrigerator until it was gone. Fortunately, Alex likes root beer so he consumed most of it.

I had just one thing to do - bring home root beer. Yet, I still managed to screw it up!

~   ~   ~

Root beer made an encore appearance just a couple of years after that graduation open house - this time with a splash.

We had gone to the grocery store and had three bags of groceries plus a 2-liter bottle of root beer. By now, we didn't drink soda on a regular basis so I think we bought this for another gathering, perhaps Thanksgiving dinner.

Like any guy, I pride myself on how much I can carry. And I like to take as few trips from the car to the house as possible. So I loaded up both hands with grocery bags and put the bottle of root beer cradled in my arm at the elbow bend, where it would be safe.

As I entered the kitchen and began putting the grocery bags on the floor, the bottle of root beer somehow slipped from my arm and dropped to the floor.

I watched as it dropped. It almost seemed like it fell in slow motion all the way to the hardwood floor. And as the bottle hit the floor, the pressure inside blew off the cap and it started spitting root beer all over as the bottle spun around and around. It looked like a spinning fireworks display, only brown and wet.

Pat is standing there too and we're both getting sprayed with root beer. And I'm laughing. She's screaming at me to make it stop. There's root beer everywhere. Do you know how far root beer can travel when it's propelled by 2 liters of carbonated pressure? It can travel really far. And it did. All the way to the sofa in the living room. All the way under the sofa in the living room. All the way to the front door. All the way to the paint store so that we could buy more paint to remove traces of it. It took six months to clean it up. We found it everywhere. Even on the ceiling! And it's sticky. Really sticky! Pat hasn't let me carry more than one item at a time since.

~   ~   ~

I'm thirsty. Anyone in the mood for a root beer?

Whoop Dee Do!

My dad had lots of one-liners he'd like to use on us kids. One-liners like:

- If he was looking at us and we said, *"What are you looking at?"* he'd say, *"Not much!"*
- Or if we asked him something about what we're going to do on vacation he'd say, *"Mind your own bee's wax."*
- Or when we wanted to ask a question and said to him *"Dad, ….?"* Before we could finish our question he'd reply, *"That's my name, don't wear it out."*
- If we questioned something, he'd say *"Don't worry about it."*
- Or if we were excited about something he'd say, *"Whoop dee do!"*

His literary skills were unparalleled.

And so were his bed-making skills. In our house, we had to make our own beds every day. And it wasn't my mom who told us we had to do it. Guess who it was. Dad. And he made sure we knew how to do it properly and to specification. Navy specification, that is. Yup, every day I had to make my bed to U. S. Navy spec. And he'd check occasionally to make sure I was doing it properly. There was zero tolerance for error or sloppy work.

But that's not what this story is about. Well, not directly anyway.

My dad did serve in the Navy. That's how he learned bed-making skills. But he also learned a few other things. He served during World War II on an LST in the South Pacific. The LST (a military acronym for Landing Ship, Tank) carried tanks and other large military hardware that could be quickly unloaded without the aid of a dock because it had a huge, gaping mouth on the front that opened up whenever the ship beached itself (like the one shown in the photo). All the tanks and stuff could then be quickly unloaded before the enemy caught on to what they were doing.

He joined the Navy in 1942 and took a machinists course at the U of Minn. When he was assigned to a ship (an LST - photo of one to the right), they put him in the engine room taking care of the ship's engines. I suppose it was an adventure sailing the South Pacific but he never talked about it. About the only thing I know is that he was discharged in 1944 for health reasons – severe asthma.

Now you might be wondering why I'm telling you all of this. Well, it's important because of what my dad did when I was a young, impressionable teenager with no knowledge of anything and no concept of how to fix stuff (some of you may remember how competent I am at fixing things now, especially plumbing).

When I was too young to drive, my dad said to me one day,

"Billy, how'd you like me to build you a go-cart?"

That surprised me because my dad was never one for doing much of anything for us except ordering us around. It also surprised me because, up to that moment, nobody in the neighborhood had a go-cart and I didn't even have a desire to get one. I'd never been on a go-cart. In fact, the only time I'd ever <u>seen</u> one was at the Ramsey County Fair. But, as it happened, he'd come across this old lawn mower. You know, the push kind that had rotating parallel blades and two wheels, except this one also had a gasoline engine. His idea was to remove the mower blades and handle and use the wheels and engine to power the go-cart. I was young and I believed him.

So he set about building this thing by attaching some boards for the seat and a couple of baby carriage wheels he found on a baby carriage in the garage for the front. He put the wheels on either end of a 2 x 4 and fastened the middle of the 2 x 4 to the go-cart. And, he attached a rope to each corner of the 2 x 4 to create a steering mechanism. I provided unskilled labor.

After it was all finished, he started it up. With the engine running, he yelled at me to hop on and start driving. I drove around the yard having the time of my life thinking, "Wow, this thing actually works!" I drove down the driveway and around mom's peonies garden, the big trees in the front and back toward the garage. Then, as I approached the garage it occurred to me. I don't know how to stop this thing. I don't remember what happened next except I'm guessing my dad came running up behind me and turned off the engine. It came to rest without injury to anyone. He said, "I guess I forgot to add a brake." After he added the brake, I drove it just a few more times. Remember, it started out as a lawn mower and you know how fast they go.

Dad

Whoop dee do!

It was not the highlight of my youth but I appreciated his efforts.

~   ~   ~

A few years later, I was into my second car, a 1954 Chevy BelAir. It was stunning. We'd found this car together and I fell in love with it the moment I saw it. It was a 2-tone turquoise and cream, six cylinder four door. I was going to be so cool driving this car. Almost immediately, I got a girlfriend. I'm certain it was because of the car. She must have found me irresistible in it.

The car did have one small problem. It burned oil – about a quart a week. I'd pull away from a stoplight and leave everyone behind me in a blue haze. It must have smelled really good!

I drove the car all the way through my senior year of high school and into my first year of college - my girlfriend, Joyce Longfellow, by my side. In fact, I was driving it on Highway 280 to class at the U of Minn. one day when I crashed into another car that made a left turn directly in front of me. We were traveling about 50 miles an hour. I had no place to go - cars to the right of me; the center median to the left. I smashed into the back end of his car. It swung around and off to the side. And my beautiful '54 Chevy was scrunched all the way back through the radiator.

When my dad arrived on the scene, he was all business. A passerby offered his name as a witness that it wasn't my fault but my dad wasn't interested. I always believed it was because he thought it was my fault, although he never accused me of poor driving. The only thing he said was, "Couldn't you have steered out of the way?" They towed my car away, back to our house.

~   ~   ~

After a short while, my dad announced that we (note the pronoun) would fix the car. And while we're at it, since it burns so much oil, we (there's that pronoun again), will overhaul the engine. Okay, sure Dad. Like <u>we</u> have all this experience rebuilding engines, much less repairing all the damage to the body. I'm sure I uttered something like, "Are you crazy? How are WE going to do THAT!" And I'm equally sure he said something like, "Mind your own bee's wax."

My car was parked, back-end to the inside, in our garage after the crash. Before we could overhaul the engine, we had to replace both front fenders, bumper and hood. He'd picked up parts from a junkyard – they were all different colors, of course. I don't recall that replacing them was a difficult task. We just un-bolted the wrecked parts and bolted on the replacements. No big deal. Once that was finished, it was time to get into the engine. First, the radiator. Again, not a big deal. Then my dad started taking stuff off like the carburetor, spark plug wires, rotor and the valve cover. He carefully put each piece on the garage floor, noting that it was my job to remember where it all went when it was time to put it all back together.

~ ~ ~

As soon as Dad took off the valve cover, it started getting interesting. As he took all these things off, he explained what they did. I was getting a hands-on, up close and personal look at the innards of a gasoline engine. I was fascinated. He showed me the intake valves and the pistons and the rings – all that stuff. And he'd learned all this while he was in the Navy. He explained why it was burning oil so badly and he said he would have the rings on the pistons replaced so that it wouldn't happen anymore. And he knew a guy that could do it for him.

I was really impressed with Dad's knowledge, ability and courage. There's no way I would have attempted anything like that. Ever.

When he got the re-ringed pistons back, we started putting everything back together. It went remarkably well. There were only a few screws left over. He told me not to worry about it. I didn't. When we added back all the fluids, he started it up and the darn thing ran. And it didn't burn any oil. I was amazed.

Whoop dee doo!

The car was great and it ran well except for one small problem. When you'd turn off the engine, the automatic transmission would vomit fluid all over the ground.

But that's another story.

What Happens Backstage, Stays Backstage

Author's Note: Language advisory. While the use of profanity is not part of my usual lexicon, you will find it in this story and so it is rated "R."

Have you ever had an argument with a spouse or partner? If so, this story is for both of you!

~   ~   ~

There's this song by Francis Nesta.[2] It's called "The Argument." It retraces a typical discussion-turned-argument. It starts like this:

> *"It begins quite harmlessly with a very minor, minor point.*
>
> *It begins with a very minor point.*
>
> *Soon the conversation has become a confrontation that requires an explanation due to misinterpretation.*
>
> *Then a growing irritation causes hyperventilation and you speculate and contemplate a quick assassination."*

A couple of years ago, a small ensemble (three couples) from my choir (South Metro Chorale) performed this song during the choir's fundraiser known as Cabaret. We had rehearsed the song many times over the course of two months and were all ready for the show.

One snowy, icy, Minnesota winter morning, four days before the show, one of our members and my song partner (Suzanne) slipped and fell at

---

[2] "The Argument." Words and Music by Francis J. Nesta. Published by Shawnee Press, Inc.

the Mall of America parking lot. In the process, she broke her glasses and cut up her face in a few spots. If I remember right, she may have even broken her cheekbone. In any case, she went to the emergency room and they put her on drugs to ease the pain while she healed.

Unfortunately, the drugs made her groggy. At our dress rehearsal, we weren't even certain she would be able to perform – she could barely stay awake much less stand without someone holding on to her.

So anyway, back to "The Argument." Suzanne decided that the show must go on – we would perform "The Argument" while she sat on a stool. She assured us she would be okay and that she could do this, even though she was so wigged out (her phrase) from all the medications she was taking that I had to help her put on her earrings.

Suzanne and Bill

Since her face was all bruised up from her fall, I also put a bandage on my head. It was all part of the act. And it fit in perfectly, since we were portraying an arguing couple.

~   ~   ~

Now, pay attention to this next bit because your understanding of backstage protocol is important to what follows.

As you might imagine, it's dark backstage. Not only that, people backstage must be silent! And, because the curtain opens from the center, no one should be standing just there because when it opens, the audience will see you and this is a big "no, no" for our production.

So, with the Cabaret show in progress, the couples group is backstage waiting for the act before us to finish up. Each of the soon-to-be-arguing couples is mentally preparing for their walk on stage and the performance of the song. All six of us stood there in silence along with

128

the stage crew while the other act is performing just on the other side of the curtain.

I'm standing next to Suzanne, holding her arm so she won't fall over. Remember, she's all wigged out on pain meds. And, I'm gently trying to nudge her away from the curtain opening. She doesn't budge. I try again, pushing a little more firmly in the direction away from the curtain opening. Still she won't move. Once more; still nothing. She's not getting my increasingly not-so-subtle hints. Finally, in the silence and in the character of the song we're about to sing, I whisper, in perfect arguing-couple fashion:

"Move the fuck over, you stupid bitch!"

She rips open with uncontrollable, out-loud laughter! She's laughing so hard, I can barely contain my own laughing while shushing her. Neither of us can stop laughing as the curtain opens. We walk on stage still chuckling, Suzanne sits on her stool and we do our song. It goes off perfectly and the audience never heard what happened backstage just before the curtain opened.

What happens backstage, stays backstage.

Purple Lights, Black Gowns and a Pink Sweater

The girl in the pink sweater sat sobbing, as I waited for my flight.

~   ~   ~

I was flying home from a very brief journey to Marion, Indiana where my first born and oldest daughter, Renee, had just graduated from Indiana Wesleyan University.

Normally, I wouldn't have even attended the ceremony. Not because I don't care. I'm very proud of Renee. And, over the past several years, we've developed an especially close, albeit long-distance, relationship. For example, my wife Pat and I were the only family members (outside of her children) who attended her wedding, even though others were invited.

Renee & Michael
September 8, 2012

But there were plenty of reasons for me to avoid this trip all together.

Reason #1. The commencement ceremony was scheduled for a weekend when I had two concerts in which to perform; specifically, Saturday evening with the Oratorio Society and Sunday with the South Metro Chorale. Concerts take a high priority for me. Just ask my youngest daughter, Tessa. I forced her to change her wedding date to avoid a concert conflict. My bad.

Reason #2. Who goes to college graduation ceremonies anymore anyway? Especially when the graduate, Renee, is 40+ years old. Even our much younger daughter Tessa didn't do "the walk," as she called it and bluntly told us that if we wanted "to go to her graduation to go ahead but I won't be there!"

Reason #3. The ceremony is in December - one of the worst times to travel, weather-wise. If we drive, we could get stranded in Nowhere, IN. If we fly, we could be stranded at an airport somewhere.

So, when Renee texts me way back in August that the date of her ceremony is December 13th, I conveniently procrastinate telling her that I'll be there. My hope was that she wouldn't press the issue and I could get out of it altogether.

One month passes . . .

I get a text from her husband, Michael.

> *"Good morning, Bill. I just wanted to encourage you with a note about Renee's graduation. Sounded like you may have a schedule conflict. Do all you can even if it's just you on a quick flight......she REALLY wants you here and has worked so hard."*

I tell Michael of my two concerts that weekend. He replies:

> *"Wow - I understand. But it would be worth it. I know she would be really disappointed if you didn't come, and would totally appreciate all your expense and effort."*

Oh, boy. The pressure's on. How can I get out of it now? I talk with my wife, Pat. I talk with choir friends. Everyone agrees. I must go, even if it's by myself.

~   ~   ~

Pat immediately takes to the computer looking for flights that will get me there at the lowest possible cost and for the briefest time period. The best option flies me to Chicago Friday morning and returns me home Saturday evening. Flying on the weekend is expensive but at least I will arrive home in time for the second concert on Sunday. I will fly first to Chicago, then to Indianapolis where I'll rent a car, drive to Marion, Indiana, check into a hotel, go to the commencement exercises, have lunch with Renee and her family, hop in the car, drive back to the Indianapolis airport, fly back to Chicago and arrive home at 10:30 PM. I'm getting tired just writing about it. I'm definitely not looking forward to this trip.

When Renee finds out I'm coming, she's almost ecstatic and adds that her mom, my ex-wife, will also be there. Oh, goody!

I dread the trip. I even dread thinking about the trip.

Getting up at 4 AM to catch a plane to Chicago. Having to navigate my way through a big city in a rental car to a place I've never wanted to go makes me anxious. And the worst of it is, I'll be alone. Because of the expense, Pat won't be traveling with me. And I'll be missing the Downton Abbey concert - something I've been looking forward to for six months. At least I'll still be able to sing in the concert Sunday.

~   ~   ~

The week arrives. I'm still not wanting to do all this traveling. I try to find a bright spot but nothing emerges. How can I change my attitude about this trip? What can I focus on to put me in a better place about it? I can think of nothing. I just don't want to go.

Thursday - Packing Day

> Get boarding pass printed. Check.

> Sign up to have flight notifications sent to my phone. Check.

> Get second boarding pass printed. Can't figure out how to do this - another reason to be nervous about this trip. How do I get boarding passes for the connecting flights? At this point, I have no idea. I guess I'll have time to figure it out in Chicago where I have a 2+ hour layover.

> Make sure I have snacks for the plane. Check.

Go to the bank for cash. Check.

Look up current TSA rules about packing liquids. Uh, oh. Don't have a one-quart bag in which to pack toothpaste and deodorant. Hope a sandwich bag will suffice. TSA can be quite strict in enforcement of the rules. Something else for me to be anxious about.

Friday - Outbound Flight

Okay, so now Friday morning arrives. Our alarm clock goes off at 4:15, exactly four hours after going to sleep the night before when I had a dress rehearsal in preparation for Sunday's concert. Pat and I eat a quick breakfast, I grab my lightly packed bag (I'll only be gone a day and a half) and head out the door. Arriving at the Minneapolis airport, I hug my wife and kiss her goodbye and enter the terminal.

Wary as I was about the traveling I had to do this weekend, the trip came with some distracting surprises. So far, everything is going along just fine. Nothing to get worried about.

There's quite a line to get through security, even at the early hour of 6:00 AM. Almost immediately, I see a rack of plastic bags and a sign reading "For your liquids - courtesy 1-quart bags." Yay! I grab one and put my liquids inside. Now, I'm legal and starting to feel a bit more relaxed.

Security doesn't take all that long and I have plenty of time before my flight so I find a spot to sit at the gate, take out my phone and check email. Nothing of interest there.

I decided that since I have all this time waiting for my flight, that I should do some serious people watching so I start profiling the other passengers to make sure there were no suspicious characters. You see, just that same week a report about the CIA's "Enhanced Interrogation Techniques" was released and there were concerns that terrorists would retaliate. And, I did spot two people who looked like they were of Arab descent. One was a woman with a young child so I figured she was safe. The other, a guy who seemed fairly well dressed. But you can never tell. I kept a close eye on him.

Two hours later, the plane starts boarding. It's crowded and the seats are cramped. Seems like every time I fly, they get tighter and tighter. We sit quietly waiting for take off. I sit there, looking out the window at the dark and damp day. Our weather in Minneapolis has been warmer than usual for December. We've seen several days of dreary, damp, dull and dark weather. And I'm told the same weather system extends to Indiana. Needless to say, I could use some sun. But it doesn't look like I'll get any this weekend.

Our flight attendant goes through her drill of telling us where all the exits are and what to do if the oxygen masks drop down as the plane begins to taxi down the runway. You know, take-offs are the best part of flying. There's a rush that comes with the sense of sudden speed. The captain hits the accelerator and off we go, climbing sharply and quickly into the murky clouds.

Suddenly, we were hit by the most spectacular sunrise (or would it be plane-rise?) as we burst through the top layer of clouds. It was breathtaking, as if our plane were an island looking out over an ocean of gray clouds to the eastern sky, sun blazing orange in front of us. I'm speechless. So this is how my journey to Indiana begins. Things are looking up (wink, wink).

When I arrived at Chicago O'Hare, I had a couple of hours to kill so I resumed my job profiling passengers (oops, I mean, people watching). I went for a coffee and snack at Starbuck's, sat down and started watching. The only thing worthy of reporting here was the woman who, after receiving her specially ordered latte, took a photo of it - not of herself or anyone else, just the coffee. I had to wonder what her Facebook page must look like.

My only other chore for Chicago was to figure out how to get a boarding pass for my connecting flight. Since I was storing my original pass on my phone, I went there first to try and figure out where or how I could get the next one. Like magic, it was already there. The only thing

I needed to do was drag my finger across the screen. I love technology. And because I had set up my reservation to notify me of flight changes, I got text messages telling me when my next flight was and what gate it was leaving from. Beautiful. Not only am I relaxed, I'm starting to enjoy the trip. Or at least, this leg of the journey.

~   ~   ~

When I arrived in Indianapolis and began walking toward the rental car area I was greeted by the most striking display of indoor lightning I've ever seen. And it came suddenly and unexpectedly, much like that sunrise in Minneapolis. The skyway over the airport road to the rental car location was well lit by multiple, round, white lights. Or at least they started out white. As I began walking across the skyway, they began flashing a multitude of colors - blue, purple, red, orange and pink. Wow! A light show right there in the airport. What fun!

I picked up my rental car and was told I had been upgraded, at no extra cost, to a Toyota Corolla. I walked to the parking garage wondering in what universe is a Toyota Corolla considered an upgrade? Makes me think the reserved car was a Yugo! Remember the Yugo? Look it up, if you don't. Here's a photo of one.

I picked up the car and set up my phone so that Siri (the woman inside my phone who talks to me - I think she's called a personal assistant, but I'm not sure) could guide me to Marion, my destination. Siri performed beautifully. She told me which exits to take, how far to the next turn off and, two-plus hours later, announced my arrival at the hotel. I was greeted by a very friendly desk clerk and went to my room which was surprising well-equipped with a refrigerator and a microwave.

By now, it was 5:00 PM Friday and, since I hadn't eaten anything substantial since breakfast, I was hungry. About a half mile down the road I'd passed a restaurant and decided to walk there just to get some exercise. The meal was unremarkable but filling. I returned to the hotel, turned on the TV and crashed. I found a station that was running "Modern Family" episodes back-to-back.

Renee had texted me that they wouldn't be arriving until about 8:00. Her mother (my ex) was not with them. She had apparently decided not to come. Yes! This trip is getting better by the minute. Renee asked if my grandson, Michael, could sleep on the sofa bed in my room. I agreed but warned her that I had a head cold and would probably be snoring. That did not dissuade her, however.

They finally arrived about 10:00. We all went to the pool area to watch my granddaughter, Abby, do some swimming. When the pool closed at 11, we went to our respective rooms. Michael hadn't gone swimming and therefore, was already in the room - watching "Modern Family." I said goodnight to him and climbed into bed hoping he'd turn off the TV soon. He didn't. He binge-watched "Modern Family" for at least 90 minutes, then changed the channel to a real-life cop show which he watched until dark-thirty. I have no idea how much, or how little, sleep I got that night.

~   ~   ~

Saturday - Graduation Day

And now the big day arrives. We've agreed to meet in the lobby after breakfast to travel, caravan-style, to the University Chapel Auditorium which is where the commencement will be held. When we arrive, I'm struck by the size of the place. The word "chapel" is deceiving. It's a very large auditorium. We soon learn that there will be 1468 students graduating this morning. My grandson, Michael, asks how long that will take. I tell him figure 5 seconds for each name to be read out-loud plus time for a couple of speeches. He's not too happy hearing this. Frankly, neither am I.

The program begins and the graduates start filing in to the sounds of Pomp and Circumstance. And, much to my surprise, I start tearing up! What the heck? Is this why I was meant to be here today? My feelings of pride and happiness overwhelmed me. My oldest daughter was graduating college after having completed the last two years under the most difficult of circumstances - raising two children and working a full time job. What an awesome achievement. Now, I'm really glad I chose to be here. This moment makes it all worthwhile.

After an address by the University President and a blessedly brief speech by the guest of honor, the awarding of degrees began. And it went like clockwork. They had a well thought-out system that worked beautifully. The entire program was finished in less than 90 minutes. We went for lunch, toasted Renee with sparkling apple cider and all headed out to return to our respective homes.

Michael, Abby, Renee, Michael

I thought the adventure was over, but . . .

~ ~ ~

The trip back to the Indianapolis airport was unremarkable. But when I arrived there, I was a bit surprised. The airport seemed a little sparse, people-wise. And it continued to get more and more sparse as my 2-hour wait continued. Now, some would say I was just overly bored but I truly saw this as an unusual phenomenon for the middle of a Saturday afternoon. So much so, I took a photo and texted it to my wife. By the way, did you know that those automated walkway announcements are queued by people walking on them? You know the one - "The automated walkway is coming to an end. Please watch your step." Yup. The announcements don't happen until someone is on the walkway. I told you I was bored!

Indianapolis Airport, Saturday afternoon.

Fast forward to the Chicago O'Hare Airport. Lots more people here. But I suppose O'Hare is always busy. I actually have a hard time finding a spot to sit.

Once I do find a spot and sit down to relax, I decide to resume my profiling (oops again - people watching) job. Almost immediately I see a young girl, 20-something. She's fingering two electronic devices, one an iPad and the other a smartphone. And, she intermittently jots notes on an old-fashioned note pad - you know, the kind made with paper. She's obviously traveling alone and is moderately interesting in that she's wearing a pea-green stocking cap, light pink sweater and a frilly, black and white mini-skirt. She also has a small, greenish tattoo under her left ear and a silver ring around her left index finger. As she's switching between smartphone, iPad and notepad, I notice that she starts sobbing. Not so loud that I could hear her, but definitely sobbing. I kind of expected the guy sitting next to her to offer some assistance but he completely ignored her. She continued to sob; people all around her.

What could be the problem? Did her boyfriend break up with her? Is she pregnant? Did a loved one die? I have no clues. Suddenly, the gate attendant calls someone to the gate. The girl gets up. I notice she's carrying a passport. Huh. She's either coming into or leaving the country. Maybe she's a terrorist and she's crying because she's afraid of blowing herself up. Nah. She's too innocent looking for that. My profiling skills have been finely tuned on this trip and I know what I'm talking about.
She approaches the gate attendant but I can't tell what they're talking about. She returns to her seat and resumes sobbing.

Later, on the plane as they're serving refreshments, the sobbing girl in the pink sweater walks past me and tries to get by the beverage cart.

It's not gonna happen so she returns to her seat in the rear of the plane. Later, when the cart is gone, she walks up again towards the front of the plane. Maybe that's where the lavatory is. Anyway, when she returns, she's no longer crying. Or not so anyone could tell. I guess I'll never know what her story is but I sure had fun wondering about it.

~   ~   ~

On the return flight from Chicago to Minneapolis, I expected no more adventures. The journey was over, or nearly so, anyway. My profiling days were done. I had nothing to do but find my seat on the plane, sit down and be quiet.

The plane was packed. People were having to check their overhead bags because they ran out of room. It was also nighttime, so after the plane took off, they turned out most of the lights. A few people were reading and so there was just a bit of light coming from those tiny overhead, personal lights. In a strange way, it seemed quite romantic; this dimly lit cabin filled with people mostly not knowing each other. I could almost imagine it being lit by candlelight and sitting there dining with my wife at this cozy little restaurant called Flight 1384.

Across the aisle and up a row was another young woman. She also wore a stocking cap but added a scarf to her ensemble. And her left knee was bouncing up and down rather quickly - sort of like a nervous twitch. Okay, so everybody does this occasionally, right? Except that she didn't stop. And her left hand lay, intermittently outstretched and clenched into a fist, on her left knee as it bounced. Huh, again. My profiling skills kicking in once more led me to deduce that she's terrified of flying. At one point, she tried to read the in-flight magazine but had to put it down presumably because she couldn't read it in bouncing mode. Her knee bounced all the way to Minneapolis. I felt bad for her and wondered if there were others on board who had the same anxieties.

~   ~   ~

And so, the trip concludes without additional drama or surprise. I arrive safely home and look forward to another flying adventure. I wonder who I'll see next time?

Ghost!

My mom's health had been declining for months. She was 87 years old and you can expect to see some aging issues anyway but it was not pleasant to witness. Since she also had increasing dementia, she was living in a memory care unit. My wife, Pat, and I visited her regularly and she always (thankfully) knew who we were.

There was one thing about Mom that never wavered - her life-long love of song. When I was younger, she taught me how to play chop sticks on the piano. In her retirement, she joined the bell choir at her church. One time when we arrived for a visit with her at the retirement center, we found her playing the lobby piano for the residents. We were pleasantly shocked. When mentioning how impressed and proud we were about 15 minutes later, she had no memory it. Wish I'd taken a photo.

I would call her on the phone every day and, even though our conversations were very limited in scope, we always ended each call with a song. And she always remembered the melody and all the lyrics. Even better then I did. In the end, song was the only way we could connect.

> *"Somewhere, over the rainbow,*
> *Way up high*
> *There's a land that I heard of,*
> *Once in a lullaby."*

~   ~   ~

As I said, Mom's health had been in steady but slow decline for several months. Officially, she was on hospice care, which provided care services (such as a hospital bed in her room along with daily visits from a nurse) over and above those provided by the memory care facility. It was May and we had planned a trip to Colorado to visit my daughter, Sarah, and her family. Weighing all the information we had available, we decided to follow through on our plans, paying a visit to Mom before flying to Denver for a long weekend. She was really out of it, barely conscious, and I don't think she even knew we were there. We gave her a forehead kiss, told her we loved her and departed.

~   ~   ~

Jason, Sarah's then significant other, now fiancé, picked us up at the Denver airport and we took the hour plus drive to their house. The mountains in the distance were mesmerizing but they couldn't compare with seeing Sarah and my grandkids Corin and Ryan, along with their dogs and cats. Lucky for us,  they were kind enough to put us up in a guest room in their home.

One of our excellent adventures on that visit was a trip to Estes Park and the haunted Stanley Hotel. The Stanley Hotel is a fascinating place which, according to folklore, abounds with ghosts.[3] Now you might pooh-pooh this idea just like I did, but I'm here to tell you, the circumstantial evidence can be quite compelling. For example, there are eye-witness accounts of the ghosts of children wandering the

---

[3] You may have seen the movie *The Shining* with Jack Nicholson. The movie was loosely based on Stephen King's book of the same name but was not filmed at the Stanley Hotel. Stephen King was inspired by his unusual and unexplained experiences while staying at the Stanley Hotel.

fourth floor hallway in the night (this is where the theme song from *Twilight Zone* starts playing in my head - do do Do do, do do Do do).

~ ~ ~

Having our interest aroused, we decided to take the Ghost Tour of the Stanley. And it was fascinating. Among other things, we learned that actor Jim Carrey had stayed there once. Something (we don't know what it was) frightened him so much in the middle of the night that he immediately checked out vowing to never return.

Sarah and Family

The hotel is a beautiful place with a stunning view of the mountains. Someday, I'd like to go back and spend a night there.

~ ~ ~

Since the hotel is near the town of Estes Park, we drove the short distance into town for a look around. It's mostly a touristy place with a river running through it. But we found a pub so decided to stop in for a beer and burgers. While enjoying our time there with Sarah and everyone, I received a phone call from my sister informing me that my mom had passed away.

At first, I was sad and started missing her. We left the bar and Sarah and I went to sit on a bench outside while the others shopped. I was in a quiet, reflective mood, not saying much.

~ ~ ~

Did I mention Mom was a dancer? I have it on good authority from Joyce Meyer, her life-long friend, that mom enjoyed the waltz and (get this) the polka! Go figure! And I'm guessing that when she met my dad, they'd go out dancing. In those days, that was the thing to do, right?

~   ~   ~

As we sat there in front of a toy store, Sarah said:

> *"Look! Didn't Gramma have one of those when we were kids?"*

I looked up and sure enough, I recognized it immediately. In the store window was a large, green, pink and yellow-feathered bird with wings and legs on strings. It was a marionette. And it was dancing!

Could it be Mom's ghost?

I knew instantly.

Whether it was her ghost or not, my mom was telling me that she was not only okay, but happy. Dancing happy!

~   ~   ~

Mom, thanks for everything you did for me, especially all the great memories – the old ones and the new ones that just keep coming!

And, I'm still singing. Can you hear me?

Dancing Mom!
(the marionette in the store window)

Appendix

Poem: The Fall of Summer

I patiently wait for fall,
My favorite season.
I wait for it all year long.

Summer wanes and the mornings become chilly.
Suddenly, the change.
The backyard explodes in reds and yellows.
Leaves commence their colorful conversion
They give up their last green breath to brown-ness and death.

But even in death there is beauty.
They say goodbye with a final sweet fragrance that permeates the air.
The first hard freeze stops everything.
The birdbath is frozen.
The planters once blooming in the joy of warm weather
Are now as brown as the leaves on the ground.

Everything is dead or dying.
On a windless, cloudy cold day,
Leaves on the hackberry tree outside my window
Fall like snow and pile up
Onto a bed of their dead comrades
Lying on the ground.

It makes me feel sad somehow.
This season I wait so patiently for
Is now creating a somber mood.

But there is also joy at fall's arrival.
Joy and sadness, too.
How can I feel both at the same time?

I thank the leaves for their summer gift.
All too soon, it's over.

About the Author

Bill Gurnon first learned of the power of personal storytelling in 1999. He studied and practiced the craft of oral storytelling with mentor, Don Forsberg, along with other storytellers in a group known as "Real Lives Aloud" in Northfield, Minnesota. The group met weekly for about ten years and performed several times in storytelling concerts at the Northfield Arts Guild Theater. Bill's oral stories were met with humbling interest and some were even recorded and subsequently aired on Twin Cities Public Television and Minnesota Public Radio.

When Real Lives Aloud disbanded and formal oral storytelling was no longer part of his weekly routine, Bill decided to transcribe his oral stories into written stories with the purpose of including them in a book for family and friends. This volume is a result of that effort.

For Bill, writing is a passion, not an educated skill. But it is without apology that he presents this book written in his own words and in his own style.

If you're interested in learning more about how you can harness the power of personal storytelling and the impact it can have on you and those around you, visit story-booker.com or contact Bill at bill@story-booker.com.

Made in the USA
Lexington, KY
05 April 2018